Minnesota Phenology

Minnesota Phenology

SEASONAL NORTHLAND NATURE

Larry Weber

NORTH STAR PRESS OF ST. CLOUD, INC.
St. Cloud, Minnesota

*To Frannie, my companion on many annual trips through nature.
And to my many students, young and old, who helped me take a
closer look at the seasonal changes and happenings in nature.*

ISBN: 978-0-87839-559-0

Printed in the United States of America

Published by
North Star Press of St. Cloud, Inc.
St. Cloud, MN

www.northstarpress.com

Contents

A Look at Phenology

PHENOLOGY IS NOT A WORD that is in everyone's vocabulary, so I need to start by defining it.

This fact hits me nearly every day, since the computer that I am using now will reject the word when I hit "spell check." Here are a couple of definitions from recent dictionaries:

> PHENOLOGY (American Heritage Dictionary): The study of periodic biological phenomena, such as flowers, breeding and migration, especially as related to climate.

> PHENOLOGY (Merriam Webster's Collegiate Dictionary): A branch of science dealing with the relations between climate and periodic biological phenomena (as bird migration or plant flowering). ca. 1884.

Unfortunately, the word may be confused with any or all of the following:

> PHRENOLOGY: The study of the conformation of the skull based on the belief that it is indicative of mental faculties and character. (This pseudoscience has often been called "the study of bumps on the head".)

> PHONOLOGY: The science of speech sounds including especially the history and theory of sound changes in a language or in two or more related languages.

> PHENOMENOLOGY: The study of the development of human consciousness and self-awareness as a preface to philosophy.

> PENOLOGY: A branch of criminology dealing with prison management and the treatment of offenders.

Also, I like to pronounce the word phenology with a long "e" to keep it from being misunderstood for these fabricated words: Fun-ology, Fin-ology or Finn-ology.

Phenology was a fairly common word and concept with people interested in natural history in the late 1800s. At the turn of the century, nature study books and nature writers were very poplar. The best known of these writers were John Muir and John Burroughs. Changing trends in the years following World War I made this science much less known. In the late twentieth century, we saw a revival in phenology. The practice rather than the word was continued by writers such as Aldo Leopold, but also was kept alive largely by observant naturalists at Nature Centers.

What We Do In the Science of Phenology

WITH MANY, PHENOLOGY IS KNOWN as a "first science". That is, phenology is seen only as noting the occurrence of first happenings of the season. This is commonly done with the arrival of migrant birds or the opening of a kind of flower, tame or wild.

This observance of firsts is no doubt part of phenology, but it goes far beyond this. The dedicated phenologist is aware of the entire passing of the season. Besides noting the migrants and wild flowers, so too are the waking of hibernators such as woodchucks, chipmunks, snakes, frogs, butterflies and bumble bees. But we also note the occurrence of egg-laying, courtship behavior, fledgling, population peaking and falling.

We observe nature through all the seasons. Yes, we watch the blooming of flowers, but also the leafing, seeding (fruiting) and passing of plants. We note the coming of and proliferation of fungi. We see the insects as they arrive, swarm, court, lay eggs and die. And the spiders as they emerge, grow, make webs, egg sacs and balloon.

And it goes beyond this. We diligently keep track of weather: temperature, precipitation (both rain and snow), sunrise and sunset times, moon phases and any other astronomical event. Instead of being a science of firsts, phenology has become a science of everything.

My Use of Phenology

I BEGAN MY OWN PHENOLOGICAL STUDIES in the early 1970s. I noted many of the seasonal changes, but it was not until I began keeping a daily nature journal on January 1, 1975, that I got deeply involved in this fascinating study. I have continued this nature journaling every day since then.

My journal writing has forced me to take a closer look at nature. When writing at least a page a day, I make note of all I saw for that day. I also keep track of the first birds, mammals, reptiles, amphibians, butterflies, dragonflies, other insects, spiders, wild flowers, tree flowers, tree leafing, leaf color change, fruits, berries, seeds and fungi that I find as I travel through the seasons. To this data, I add the dates of thawing, freezing, high and low temperatures, winds, precipitation, moon phases and sunrise and sunset times.

For more than thirty-five years, I have also written a second journal, where I take one phenomenon of the day and take a closer look at it. This journaling has given me a grasp of the moment, made me more aware of nature, and I feel good about each day.

Looking back at about forty years of nature journal keeping, more than 14,000 days, I feel that I have not only gotten a grasp of seasonal nature, I have even felt its pulse. I know what is happening around me and even what is about to happen. I've been able to look beyond the arrivals of migrants and the awakings of spring to see their growth of summer and maturity of autumn. I have observed the countless organisms (critters) that live amongst us and travel this cycle with us. And when problems and stresses arise in my life, I take a walk to see what's happening in our woods, fields, ponds, swamps and streams. Seeing all the nature news here puts everything in its proper place.

I have been able to show my students that despite all the less-than-desirable human news, the news in the world of nature, the real news of life, is always notable and interesting. Using phenology in my classroom has added years to my teaching career and my youth.

Phenology and My Teaching

WHEN ASKED TO DEVELOP and teach a seventh grade science curriculum in the early 1980s, I decided to look at putting phenology in the classroom. The result was a phenology-based natural science class that has thrived for twenty-five years.

We use no written textbook. Rather, the seasons became our text. We study whatever was going on in nature at that time of year.

In the classroom, we note the weather for each day, including the high and low temperatures, precipitation amounts (snow and rain) and winds. Daily temperatures are plotted and monthly precipitation results are recorded. At the beginning of each month, we list and discuss what will happen in the coming month. We also look at the times of the moon phases for the month and other astronomical events. We discuss the month names and try to come up with more meaningful names of our own. We use fall and spring phenology charts, where we record the first and last sighting of common local flora and fauna. Students are regularly given time to share their own findings, either as sights (critter news) or a caught specimen brought in, examined and talked about but always released quickly thereafter.

Regularly, every week or two, we choose a topic pertinent to what is happening in nature at that time of year. This topic is introduced and discussed indoors, then followed by a walk outdoors to see the same phenomenon. These topics continue throughout the entire school year. We have looked at raptor migrants, wild flowers, fungi, insects and spiders in fall; animal tracks and signs, winter birds and plants in winter; and tapped maple trees, visited frog ponds, wild flowers and songbird migrants in spring. With all this material properly done, the students get a look at the local flora and fauna along with the seasonal changes. They see that nature is alive and active here and now, not always somewhere else at another time.

Trends Over the Past Forty Years

I AM FREQUENTLY ASKED if I have seen phenological changes during this period of time. Over the years, I have noticed that some of the arrivals and awakenings of spring make good phenology indicators. The best ones are those that are easy to observe (large, colorful or loud). When they are here, we take notice. Some good spring indicators are: red-winged blackbirds, tundra swans, ovenbirds, Baltimore orioles, rose-breasted grosbeaks, chipmunks, woodchucks, wood frogs (calling), bumble bees, spring azures, tiger swallowtails, field crickets, orb-web spiders, alder catkins, bloodroots, marsh marigold, trout-lilies, large trilliums, wild plums and morels.

These are easy to see, common and consistent. The locating or first sights of many others may be more sporadic or influenced by other factors. An example of this is the decline of spring peepers in my area. Though still heard in April, they are much fewer than a few years ago, due to a deep freeze that we experienced in the winter of 2002-2003. Likewise, pussy willows, seen by many as a harbinger of spring, opened in late January of 2006. Robins and juncos, still acclaimed by many as signs of spring, have often wintered in the northland.

I have also noticed a longer season. The ice seems to be leaving earlier from area lakes. The early spring wild flowers, formerly seldom seen before April 20, may now be a week before this time. And some migrants are now arriving here earlier. Are these signals of the warming trend we hear so much about?

This might be true, but it may also be due to some other factors. I may have gotten better at finding the spring phenomena, or I may have discovered a particular site where they are easy to see. Results are best seen if we record the same place each year and we look at the entire phenology and not just the first occurrence.

Whether or not we are looking for phenological indicators of global warming, watching the natural changes as the seasons go by is just plain interesting. It teaches us to be better observers of nature. It makes every day unique. To quote the great naturalist John Burroughs, "If you want an adventure in nature, take the same walk that you took yesterday, and do so again tomorrow." Perhaps we too can be as skilled as Thoreau whose friend Emerson said about him, "He thought that if waked up from a trance, in this swamp, he could tell by the plants what time of year it was within two days."

Using This Book

I USE THE MONTHS as the basis of the year. Months are well known, convenient to use and a natural time indicator. The word "month" comes from the word "moon," and the number of days in a month is nearly equal to that of the lunar cycle. I have given the source of our common names of the months, but I also list the local Native American names and some phenological names as well (based on consistent phenomena of that time of year). Looking further at the month, I have listed various happenings that are likely to be observed in the early, middle and late times of month. These can and will vary with different years, but are listed since they have often appeared at these times in my decades of keeping a nature journal. These are accurate and good indicators of the changing seasons, but the list is far from complete. For each month, I have also provided a series of essays with photos of some phenological happenings that I have observed over the years. And I give a summary of what each month has to offer.

The weather statistics given for each month are based on the measurements for the National Weather Service at Duluth, Minnesota. Professionally done and recorded for more than one hundred years, these data can be used as indicators of weather in the western Great Lakes region and the North Woods. Average weather statistics are taken from the National Weather Service and are based on thirty year records and are updated each decade. The one in use in this book are from the statistics of 1980-2010.

The eight essays for each month are taken from hundreds that I wrote as weekly nature columns for a Duluth, Minnesota newspaper. Though far from complete for each month, they do give a look at varied local flora and fauna during the applied month.

This book is meant to be an introduction to the observational science of phenology for the upper Midwest, western Great Lakes and the North Woods. It is not a complete guide to the seasonal changes of everything in the outdoors. Gardeners, farmers, hunters and anglers may feel much is being left out. The book is a fine help to the nature watchers who like to visit favorite outdoor sites or who regularly go for walks. I hope it will stimulate an interest to look at nature more closely, no matter where you live and no matter what you enjoy doing in the outdoors.

I encourage any nature observer to keep a journal of your own and make note of any of your findings. The trip through the year is a marvelous journey enjoy and keep the fun (phun) in phenology.

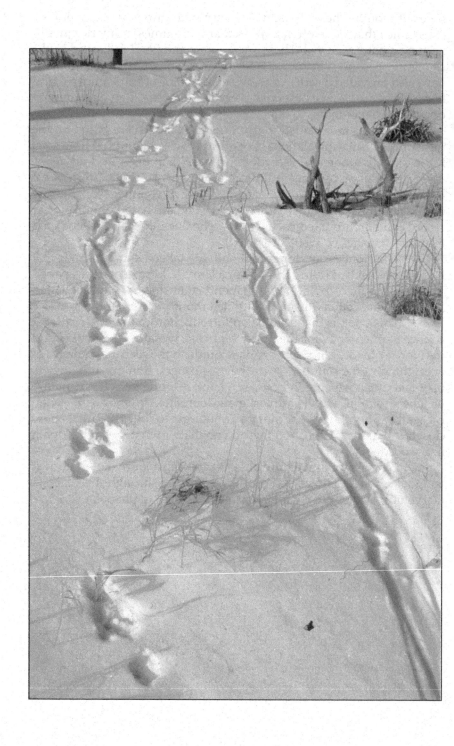

January

JANUARY GETS ITS NAME from Janus (Ianuarius), the god of the doorway. As the first month of the year, January can be seen as the door to the New Year.

GICHI MANIDOO GIIZIS:
The Great Spirit Moon

PHENOLOGICAL NAMES:
The Cold Month
The Snowy Month
The Month of Perihelion

J ANUARY IS A FRIGID WAKE-UP to the New Year. It is both the coldest and often the snowiest month, a bitter reminder of Minnesota's north-country status as the mercury dips to thirty below zero. We find it hard to believe that the Earth is closest to the sun in our annual orbit (perihelion). January sees slowly lengthening days stretching into lingering sunsets blending with the brightest full moon of the year.

January is all about deep snows, thick ice, and subzero temperatures. Cold and wind are the norm, with at least one large snow storm where weather forcasters speak of "blizzard." Bitter nights can nudge records that many hardy northlanders pride. But January also usually has a few days of thaw.

In January a morning walker can hear trees cracking and snow crunching with each step—sometimes the only sounds. But just as we wonder if any animals live in such conditions, a croaking raven soars overhead. January landscapes appear empty and devoid of life. Bare trees stand against a backdrop of white with only the conifers lending color to the scene. The month looks to the future as hardy lichens cope with the chill and the seeds of flowering plants formed last summer sleep above the snow, begging for animal or wind dispersal.

A plethora of tracks appear in the snow blanket each morning. In the deep powder, we read the neighborhood nocturnal news, follow the hungry hunts of coyotes in the fields, pine martens and ermine scampering after meals in the woods, and hare and porcupines nibbling among the downed branches.

Voles and shrews live under the snow as beaver and muskrats live under the ice. Deer yard up, raccoons sleep, and woodchucks hibernate. Scent markings tell of the foxes and coyotes nearing the new breeding season. And newborn bear cubs snuggle with their sleeping moms.

January is a time of hungry birds. The short days are spent eating to warm their tiny bodies. Crossbills break open cones, waxwings work on frozen berries. Feeders are active with chickadees, nuthatches, and grosbeaks devouring sunflower seeds while goldfinches, siskins, and redpolls go for thistle seeds. Woodpeckers attack the suet.

Hungry shrikes at the feeder too, as predators seek seed eaters. Wintering owls search out small mammals in deep snow. January is hunger, cold, and storms while longer days bring us to midwinter and slow steps towards the warming times.

January Happenings: The Cold Month

What to look for:

Early January
- black-capped chickadees, boreal chickadees, redpolls
- tracks in deep snow
- insect galls
- moth cocoons
- conifer trees

Mid January
- ravens
- ruffed grouse in deep snow
- gray squirrels at feeders
- shrews under the snow
- tansy, mullien hold seeds above the deep snow
- cattail seeds
- parmelia and xanthoria lichens on trees

Late January
- hawk owls
- crossbills
- skunks active in the thaw
- wolves and coyotes begin breeding
- black bears birthing
- deer yarding
- wingless winter crane flies walking on snow -beard lichens

PERIHELION

ACH YEAR IN EARLY JANUARY, we experience the beginning of the New Year. Along with hopes, plans, and resolutions, we start another annual trip. The year, being our orbit around the sun, is actually cyclic and as such, has no beginning nor ending, just a continuous travel through the seasons. We mark the passing of time by natural occurrences of sunlight and darkness (days) and moon phases (months). Weeks are a human invention and its length is not based on natural cyclic events. Our journey around the sun takes a bit longer than 365 days, and we need to adjust our calendar with leap years every four years. And since our path is cyclic, we could designate any date as the beginning of the year. We do this in many ways. Each of us has our own new year's day on our birthday. We begin tilling, planting and harvesting at certain times, and sports seasons have beginning and ending dates as well. Those of us who were involved in education considered the first day of school as our new year's day.

Many nature watchers claim that the year actually commences with the vernal equinox, the first day of spring, in March. Indeed, our calendar formerly did use March 1 as the year's starting point. This explains why September, October, November, and December are named after these respective numbers: seven, eight, nine and ten, pointing to which month of the year they were, even though they don't occupy those positions on the modern calendar. It also explains why February is shorter, the last month of the year had two days taken from it, placed in other months: July and August. The choice of January 1 as the beginning is a bit of an arbitrary date and appears not to be based on any events going on in nature. What could be happening in the natural world at this time that might cause us to consider it a new year? This is, however, a time of several natural changes. About ten days ago, we marked the winter solstice and subsequently, the days slowly begin to get longer. Sunsets are later, and Sol rises earlier each day. But for me, the greatest event of the new year is the perihelion.

Our route around the sun is not a perfect circle. Instead it is an ellipse — we are not at the same distance away from the sun at all times. The ninety-three million miles is an average distance, approximated on the equinoxes of March and September. We reach a point most distant from the sun (aphelion) in early July. When we are nearest (perihelion) is now, early January! The exact date of perihelion varies from January 1 to January 5, but it usually occurs on the second, third, or fourth. This year perihelion is on January 3 at about 1:00 P.M. Even though we who live in the northern hemisphere are closer to the source of heat at this time, we are in the midst of winter and experiencing some of the coldest temperatures of the whole year. This paradox is due to our planet being tilted, the sun's rays hit the northern hemisphere at a lower angle. The southern hemisphere is hit more directly, and they are in a hot summer now.

I think that the new year starting with perihelion is very natural and a good time to begin. Our ancestors who chose January 1 as the start did so with less astronomical knowledge than we have, so it may be just a coincidence that it coincides with perihelion, but marking the beginning of a journey with our closest encounter to the sun is a good place to begin. Happy New Year; enjoy the trip!

BLACK-CAPPED CHICKADEES

RECENT SNOWS AND COLD weather have made this time feel truly like the winter season that began with the solstice on December 21. Whether seen as recreation or drudgery, the snow and cold impacts our days. We are not alone in being influenced by this change. Birds, along with the local squirrels, are making more use of our feeders now. Though nature has provided plenty of food for these feathered neighbors in the woods, fields, and marshes, the ease of snacking in our yards brings them here during the chill. Despite what is often thought, the wintering avian crowd can do very well without us during this cold and dark season. They do not need us, but maybe we need them.

Many a winter day has been more delightful for us as we watch the nuthatches, woodpeckers, grosbeaks, blue jays, siskins, and redpolls feeding and moving with the excitement of a warmer time. However, none can match that of the tiny black-capped chickadees.

Often the first sign of life on frigid winter mornings, these hardy birds shrug off the cold to pick up their feeding where they left off the day before at dusk. Looking just as they did the previous summer, their four-and-one-half-inch gray bodies sport black caps and bibs as they greet the new day.

After cold winter nights spent alone in trees, they arrive at the feeder with the dawn and flit there off and on until dusk, even while the snow is falling. If the day is severely cold, they'll fluff out their feathers to trap body heat, making these diminutive birds appear fatter than they are. Other chickadees arrive, and though they are not flocking birds, a dozen or more may visit the feeders during a winter day.

Wintering chickadees gobble sunflower seeds, suet, and peanut butter to maintain a daytime body temperature of 104 degrees. Often they'll pound away at the seeds with tiny, but powerful beaks as they sit on nearby tree branches. Uneaten seeds are frequently cached in surrounding trees in cracks and crevices known

7

only to them. These winter stores may provide a meal at a later, leaner time. This behavior, of course, was in place long before bird feeders provided steady nutrition, but should a feeder go empty and not noticed, the birds have backup.

Chickadees get their name from a common call they make, often with a repeated ending: "Chick-a-dee-dee-dee." Such calls come when we are near and disturb them. Occasionally, if the winter day is clear and mild, they may also be heard to sing a "fee-bee" song that is usually associated with spring.

As we begin the new year, let's sit a spell and watch the cheerful antics provided by these and other wintering northland neighbors at our bird feeders. Whatever it costs us to keep the birds fed and near the house is returned in abundance by their cold day performances.

BASSWOOD SEEDS

IN EARLY JANUARY, real winter has set in. Several mornings in a row, we northlanders wake to temperature readings in the sub-zero range. Talk is often of the morning chill we all are experiencing. This cold time combined with the snowpack left from the earlier storm makes for a great Minnesota winter scene.

Birds fluff up their feathers and add extra meals to their daily routine to cope with the weather. Many mammals slow their activities. Some, such as raccoons and skunks, even sleep through the chill, waking on milder days. During my walks at minus twenty, I hear the crunch with each step as my boots grind the rough snow. Ice crystals collect around my face, and I return with a frosty hat, coated in the moisture freezing from each breath. On such walks, we may have thoughts of spring, but it can be hard to see some signs. However, even in these harsh conditions, nature is in preparation for the warmth of the next season!

As I travel about on these days, whether on foot or by car, I see trees laden with seeds. Most obvious are mountain-ash, crab apple, hawthorn, sumac, and highbush cranberry that still hold reddish berries, but they're not alone. Birches, box elder, ash, and basswood all bear brown seeds on their winter branches. Sometimes the crop is so thick, these trees appear to have leaves. Not only do they foreshadow spring when these seeds may take root, but they speak of a fruitful past.

Last summer was an excellent time for seeds, berries, and fruits in the northland. Much of this was seen in the bountiful harvest we enjoyed. Other plants show the results of the previous season. I saw this on a walk as I wandered through the snowy woods after a recent snowfalls. The deep snowpack had crusted but was subsequently covered by light powdery snow. Spread out on this new white coat was an abundance of tiny birch seeds. These minute three-pointed structures had a scattering of strange-looking basswood seeds with them.

Basswoods—rather large trees that blend in with maples and oaks in our woods—have diagnostic large heart-shaped leaves. But they flower in the summer, not in spring like most other trees. Basswoods open their clusters of flowers in the warmth of late July. The blossoms of July 2009 were outstanding. Dripping with nectar, they attracted large numbers of bees. Several times, I walked by basswoods that literally buzzed as myriads of these busy insects gathered food from the numerous flowers.

Pollinated by these bees, the trees produced the unusual fruits now seen on the surface of the snow or still clinging to the branches. Fruits are spherical nuts nearly one-fourth inch in diameter. About four to six are attached to small stems that lead to a large single leaf-like wing. Taking advantage of winter winds hitting the exposed branches, the seeds drift on these "hang-glider" growths. Though now is cold winter with plenty of snow, the basswoods send out their seeds in hope and preparation for the months ahead. And we will continue to see these strange seeds on the snowpack in weeks to come.

COYOTES' MATING SEASON BEGINS

MID JANUARY IS A LONG WAY from spring and more closely associated with mid-winter. Days are still cold and there is plenty of snow cover, even during a mild and dry season. But signs show that the season is moving on. Quietly, the days have been getting longer. The sunset that was at 4:20 P.M. in early December is now nearly 5:00 P.M. Sunrises that reached their latest time around New Year's Day at 7:55 A.M. are now about ten minutes earlier. Indeed, the days that gave us eight and a half hours of light a month ago now have nearly nine and a half hours. Using this light lengthening, some northland wildlife respond with spring-like activities.

In the world of wild canines, this is a time of mating and pre-mating behaviors. Foxes are beginning to make their rounds regularly as are their larger cousins, the coyotes and wolves. With the limited snow cover this year, their movement is much easier, and their tracks and scent marking are easy to see. Of these three members of the dog family, the coyotes are most into the mating season at this time. With a gestation of about eight to nine weeks and pups usually born in late March or early April, they now proclaim their territories and move about regularly. During many of these cold nights of mid to late January we can hear their yipping calls as well.

A very widely dispersed critter, the coyote is about the only of the North American mammals that now has a bigger range than it did one hundred fifty years ago. Formerly a predator of the prairies and deserts, coyotes have used their cunning and intelligence to spread out, and now live over most of the country, being found in nearly every state.

While in most of their range, they remain separated from the wolves, the two species do cross territories. The northland is one of the few places where they may co-exist. Traveling far afoot through the fields, woods, swamps, and even the yards of suburbia, they are able to cope with our winters quite well. Coyotes are often heard in the region, more than seen.

Now they seek winter meals as they wander their territory and get ready for the next generation of spring. But they are not alone. Other mammals are or will soon start mating or pre-mating behavior of their own. Squirrels, rabbits, hares, foxes, wolves, and mice will be forming homelands and beginning families while the black bears celebrate a mid-winter birthing of cubs.

Yes, we are in the middle of the cold season, but thanks to the longer days, some spring things are happening.

RUFFED GROUSE IN DEEP SNOW

ITH AMPLE SNOWFALLS by this time of winter, the northland is again seeing a January covered with a thick snowpack. Normally at this time of January, we have at least a foot of snow on the ground, some places claiming about twice as much. Not only do snow sports flourish now, but the landscape is outstanding. Besides the snow cover, conifers remain cloaked in coats of recent snowstorms, thus giving an impressive scene.

The local wildlife appears to be coping with the winter snowpack quite well. The many inches of snow may cause problems, but it can also prove a benefit for many.

A few days after each additional snowfall, we read of activities in the latest set of tracks. Squirrels, rabbits, hare, foxes, coyotes, deer, weasels, martens, and fishers continue their movements. Many go over the snow while others select a route for a trail and continue traveling on these winter highways. Still others, like the mice and shrews, use the white blanket to their advantage by moving through the cold months in relative ease under the snowpack.

Survival in northland winters often depends on using what is available to cope with circumstances. Critters wintering here demonstrate this ability. Whether they face a change of diet, habits, or denning sites, they adapt to the scene. Such is the case of the ruffed grouse, which take advantage of January's deep snows to ward off the chill of a cold snap. The birds need enough snow to bury themselves under three or four inches of it. Flying straight into the snow, they proceed to form burrows. The typical scenario involves plunging into the snow, burrowing a few feet to create a shelter, sleeping the night, then exploding out the next day. Once while I was snowshoeing at Jay Cooke State Park, the snow erupted where I was about to step as a sheltered grouse took leave when I got too close.

Their tracks and wing marks on the forest snow are a common winter sight to those of us who walk the woods in January. Prolonged inclement weather can keep these grouse holed up for several days of hungry safety.

13

Not only is the burrow a shelter from predators, but snow acts as an insulator for the grouse, allowing them to spend the night in a climate perhaps thirty degrees above the outside air temperature. Snow is, in fact, a wonderful insulator.

When proper snow for burrowing cannot be found, birds form "snow bowls" on the surface or settle into conifers for the night. During the milder days that often come during winter, grouse will be out visiting shrubs and trees for meals of buds and berries before weather causes them to take another burial beneath the snow.

WALKING AT MINUS THIRTY

I NEED TO SHINE A LIGHT on the thermometer during this hour of pre-dawn darkness, but it's plain to see that the morning is quite cold — minus thirty! Many would refrain from a walk at this temperature, but this is also part of the season and worth getting out to take a closer look. Well prepared, I step outside.

Going down the driveway to the road, where I will do most of my walking, I see the fresh tracks of a cottontail rabbit showing me that this critter, which has been surviving the winter in the yard, has been active despite the cold. Out along the road, I quickly note that I'm bathed in the bright light of a near-full moon, just past its peak, but still very bright in the west. Luna's glow is enhanced with the reflection off the new snow cover. My path is illuminated by this phenomena. In this lit scene, though the sky is crystal clear, constellations are dimmed, hard to see, but Venus shows her glow in the east even as early rays from the winter sunrise are creeping over the horizon. In the chill, I hear only the crunchy sounds of my footsteps on the frozen snow and an occasional *crack* from a tree as some residual sap expands in ice, causing an explosive adjustment.

I'm able to discern more along the road. Hoofed prints tell me a deer has wandered here too. With a snowpack of nearly two feet, deer find it easier to walk along the roads than in the deep woods. And I see movement that tells me I'm not alone. A small dark figure pushes through the inch-deep new snow along the road's edge. It appears energetic and in a hurry . . . and completely oblivious of me. I stand and watch as it gets close. I'm able to identify it as a short-tailed shrew. The largest and most common of our several species of shrews, it remains active all winter, and even at minus thirty, the shrew needs to locate food. Finding no meals at this site, it quickly departs into the deeper snow where the subnivean space is likely to offer more.

Near halfway into my two-mile walk, I note more snow messages. Even though this is cold January, I see signs that coyotes are in their mating season. At one location, I find scent markings where

15

a coyote is telling others that this territory is taken. And at another place, I see where a pair of the canines has crossed the road together.

The sun continues its rise as I begin the walk towards home and warmth. Frost has formed around my face. I know the reluctant mercury has not risen much. But critters are starting to stir. A croaking raven flies over, acting as undeterred by the cold as they seem to be by anything else. Movement in some roadside alder turns into a flock of redpolls breakfasting on the seeds. These hardy tiny birds have been avoiding my feeder, but it's nice to know they are here.

As I approach the house, sunlight has taken over the moon's glow. Fluffed-up chickadees, nuthatches, and woodpeckers have arrived at the feeders for the new day. It's still cold, but what a great winter morning I've been witnessing, and I find it satisfying that northland nature is coping with the chill.

SHREW MOVEMENTS IN WINTER

L OOKING AT THE SECOND HALF of January, we see a scene of deep winter. Our snowpack is about twenty inches for much of the northland. Recent temperatures have regularly been in the subzero range. Winter winds have provided wind chills that make the northland famous. Statistically, this time of January may be the coldest time of the whole winter. Despite these conditions, many critters continue to remain active. They deal with the cold in varied ways. Resident birds switch from a warm-weather diet of insects to seeds and fruits now available. Their feathers fluff up to provide a thicker insulation, and they devour as much food as they can to keep up their body temperature.

Other critters, such as raccoons and skunks, curl up in their hidden dens to sleep through the coldest times. Snowshoe hares use large feet to climb over the new-fallen snow to find twig treats higher up than they could otherwise reach. Ruffed grouse take advantage of the snow itself as a shelter and home. And they are far from alone in doing this. Beneath the many inches of white lies a labyrinth of small mammal tunnels. The best known makers of these, the field mice or voles, may have a maze of trails that extend hundreds of feet in this subnivean space. Here they pass the cold days in relative ease—warmer than in the exposed places and safely hidden from many predators. Trapping the geothermal heat (that given off from deep within the Earth), snow acts as a blanket. On January days the temperature is often forty to fifty degrees warmer under a snowpack of twenty inches that the air above. Voles find plenty of food, the seeds and stems of meadow plants. Conditions are so good they often breed while still under the snow. We usually are not aware of the tunnels until spring, but occasionally their finger-sized "vole holes" appear on the surface.

Such populations are sought as food by winter predators. Least weasels—ermine—and shrews are able to work their way into this meadow mouse paradise and find plenty to pounce upon. Though weasels are a bit uncommon here, shrews are quite com-

17

mon. Five kinds of these small energetic mammals live in the region. The most abundant is the short-tailed shrew. Only about three inches long with a one-inch tail, these dark-gray critters have a voracious appetite.

Active (or maybe hyperactive) all year long, they also seem to be just as willing to hunt in daytime as night. Summertime is spent feeding mostly on worms, insects, spiders, and other residents of the soil (animals or plants). Winter's diet takes on more of a flavor of seeds and berries, but a mouse meal is a desired change. They are successful predators even if the mouse is bigger than they are. Though they live in our yards, meadows, and woods, we are not likely to see them as they move about under the snow. Sometimes, however, their trails cross ours, and we see them scamper over sidewalks and streets as they travel the snow's subsurface in a quest for food.

Unfortunately, many northlanders refer to shrews as moles. Though cousins of moles, shrews are much smaller and look quite different from our most common mole: the star-nosed mole. It can be a long hungry winter for this tiny mammal with the big appetite. No doubt, many do not make it through the winter, but enough are able to live under the snow to survive the cold and sustain a healthy population in the northland.

WINTER LICHENS

ANY OF THE LOCAL FLORA and fauna that live through a northland January must be hardy, like wintering birds and mammals that remain active all season. They might vary their diet from what they ate during the warm times, but such changes and adaptations are needed to survive the cold.

Others go dormant either below the snow and frost or right out in the open. Probably the most obvious example of this stoic exposure to the chill can be seen in the trees themselves. We are surrounded by both the deciduous and coniferous trees that appear to do nothing all winter, often looking like they are dead, but they are dealing with winter in their own way.

On their bark and branches, crusty, wrinkled or stringy growths of lichens deal with winter too. These lichens, also found growing on bare rocks, just may be the hardiest of any living things in the northwoods. What appears to be a single organism is actually a combination of two: algae and fungi. Tiny ball-shaped cells of algae provide chlorophyll that makes food from sunlight in the way of all plants. These cells are next to threads of fungi that hold the moisture needed for the process. This remarkable symbiosis creates growths that can thrive in nearly any environment on Earth (including Antarctica). Ironically, lichens are quickly killed in the presence of pollution.

One of the most unusual lichens in the northland is easy to see on these winter days. Hanging from branches of dead or leafless cedars, tamaracks, and spruces in bogs are the long stringy or hairlike lichens known as old man's beard. Greenish-gray, this "beard" lichen dangles from the branches much like the Spanish moss that drapes oak trees in the South, which is not a lichen. The term "moss" is also used as a name for some reindeer lichens, but neither this lichen nor the Spanish moss is a true moss. The latter is even a type of flowering plant. Some beard lichen (*Usnea*) can reach a length of two to three feet, though most of what we see on bog trees is much shorter.

Unlike other lichens that grow flat on a surface, old man's beard hangs from branches, a substrate to hold onto. This gray-green lichen does not hurt the trees. On dead branches, it finds sunlight even among the dense-needled conifers and is able to make the needed food and gather moisture to survive winter.

Often only in winter can the lichen be seen clearly. Though bogs may be deep in snow and travel there may be difficult, those who snowshoe, skis or snowmobile can easily see this hanging lichen. In some bogs, it seems like every available dead cedar, tamarack, or spruce has a growth of old man's beard lichen draped on it.

Daily Climate Information for Duluth, Minnesota

Normals Records

Day	Average High	Average Low	Record High	Record Low	Sunrise	Sunset
1	19	3	43/1897	-30/1974	7:54	4:31
2	19	3	45/1889	-41/1885	7:54	4:32
3	19	2	42/1899	-30/1911	7:54	4:33
4	19	2	38/1992*	-29/1884	7:54	4:34
5	19	2	48/2012	-32/1912	7:53	4:35
6	19	2	45/2012*	-34/1909	7:53	4:36
7	19	2	46/2003	-36/1912	7:53	4:37
8	19	2	48/2003	-31/1974	7:53	4:38
9	19	2	45/2012	-38/1875	7:53	4:40
10	19	1	47/2012	-36/1912	7:52	4:41
11	19	1	42/1986	-35/1912	7:52	4:42
12	19	1	45/1987	-34/1912	7:51	4:43
13	19	1	48/1894	-34/1929	7:51	4:45
14	19	1	51/1894	-38/1965	7:50	4:46
15	19	1	42/1933	-39/1972	7:50	4:47
16	19	1	42/1942	-31/1982	7:49	4:48
17	19	1	45/1884*	-38/1982	7:48	4:49
18	19	1	44/1891	-33/1994	7:47	4:51
19	19	1	44/1900	-32/1994	7:47	4:53
20	19	1	46/1908*	-35/1996	7:46	4:54
21	19	1	45/1900	-33/1883	7:45	4:55
22	19	1	55/1942	-35/1883	7:44	4:57
23	19	1	55/1942	-38/1935	7:43	4:58
24	19	1	50/1892	-37/1904	7:42	4:59
25	19	1	47/1973	-31/1904	7:41	5:01
26	19	1	47/1877	-31/1972	7:40	5:02
27	20	2	46/1906	-33/1885	7:39	5:04
28	20	2	51/1877	-37/1966	7:38	5:05
29	20	2	46/1877	-35/1951	7:37	5:07
30	20	2	44/1890	-35/1994	7:36	5:09
31	20	2	48/1892	-33/1982	7:34	5:10

*Denotes latest of multiple years
Average Temperature for January: 10.2 F
Average Precipitation for January: 0.96 inches
Average Snowfall for January: 19.4 inches

FEBRUARY

FEBRUARY GETS ITS NAME from the Latin word *"februum"* meaning "purification." February was the time of a purification ritual in the old Roman calendar.

NAMEBINI GIIZIS:
The Sucker Moon

PHENOLOGICAL NAMES:
The Dry Month
The Month of an Early Thaw
The Month of Lengthening Days

FEBRUARY IS USUALLY OUR DRIEST MONTH with light arid snows that bring us the least snowfall of any winter month. February's cold is capable of record setting, and its warmth of forty or fifty degrees makes slush that often refreezes. February has crusty snow, and it often drapes from the trees.

February days lengthen as the sun moves along its northern journey. Nine and half hours of daylight on the first grows to eleven by the end of the month.

Valentines, Presidents' Day, Ash Wednesday, and leap day (occasionally). February watches winter sports slow down and spring training speed up. Snowmobiling and skiing continue while ice fishing ends and snowshoeing begins.

February sees a change in the bird life around the house. Pine grosbeaks, with us through the chill of January, now slowly move north. Chickadees stay active at the feeder singing their "fee-bee" call. Woodpeckers drum and redpoll flocks become restless. The mourning dove's plaintive call is drowned out by early migrating crows. The first horned larks and snow buntings come to open fields, showing us that February is not too early to move north. Great gray, hawk and snowy owls from the far north visit us along the roadsides in hungry hunts, while resident barred and great horned owls begin breeding. The croaking of the ever-present ravens greet the screeching of starling flocks.

This is the mating season for fox, wolf, squirrels, and hare, while bear cubs grow with their slumbering mothers. Groundhogs sleep. We can see animal autographs written on light snows covering the crust. Each morning we read of the nocturnal adventures of mice, rabbits, weasels, porcupines, and signs of the recently-awaken skunks and raccoons.

Snow melts at the base of trees as dark bark absorbs the heightening sunlight and radiates it to the ground. We gather bright red-osier dogwood branches and pussy willow buds as treatments for cabin fever.

Crane flies, spiders, and springtails become active on the snow, while early emerging stoneflies and caddisflies rise from the opening streams.

February is our shortest month that paradoxically becomes the longest for the winter weary. We so want to turn towards spring.

FEBRUARY HAPPENINGS: THE DRY MONTH

What to look for:

EARLY FEBRUARY
- redpolls
- gray Jays
- red foxes, coyotes
- red squirrel tunnels
- box elder seeds
- rock and tree lichens

MID FEBRUARY
- goshawk
- barred owls
- hawk owls
- fishers, wolves
- winter scopionflies
- birch seeds on snow

LATE FEBRUARY
- woodpecker drumming
- crow flocks
- great horned owls
- great gray owls
- horned larks
- cardinals singing
- early mating behavior of squirrels
- early mating behavior of rabbits
- red-osier dogwoods
- pussy willow buds

BEAR CUBS

IT'S EARLY FEBRUARY. According to the calendar, this is mid-winter, and it can still get quite cold, as we may recall from the recording setting day of February 2, 1996. Although we do not have the minus sixty degrees experienced that day in the north or the minus forty in many places a bit further south, winter's grip is still tight upon us and will continue for some time.

Perhaps because of these weather conditions, we now have a desire to see the season pass on. Some ask a sleeping prophet, the groundhog for a weather prediction. There may be no animal that gets more attention while sleeping than does this rodent each February 2.

Groundhog Day gives publicity for a rather unglamorous animal, though it did make a good movie. Through a series of superstitious stories and misidentifications, this critter, also know as woodchuck, has been given powers it neither possesses nor needs. We ask this marmot for a sign of the coming spring, but it just continues its deep sleep of winter. However, what is happening to another animal also in a deep sleep, the mother black bear, gives hope of the coming warmer weather. In the northland, most of us have had some experiences, maybe unpleasant, with these bruins, since they frequently live near us.

All fall, bears wandered, which often bring them to the cities, to find the food needed to build fat reserves to last through the long winter sleep. Unlike the groundhog, whose hibernation is a true torpor, bears settle into their dens, but their body temperature doesn't drop as much as the rodent's does. The bear's sleep is spaced with waking periods and even some moving, although they seldom leave the four-foot sleeping site, usually beneath overturned trees, in hollow stumps, caves, thickets or even just under available conifers.

For the mother bear (sow), sleep is interrupted in late January or early February every other year for a special reason, birth. After a seven-month gestation, she gives birth during a drowsy waking time in mid winter. Born helpless and blind, the infant bears sleep and nurse until they emerge from the den with their mother in the spring. Mother bear's thick layer of fat helps her through hibernation, pregnancy, and nursing. And it provides heat that keeps the cubs from freezing through these first chilly months of life.

Two or three babies compose the usual litter size. Seven inches long and weighing only ten ounces, the cubs are a mere handful, miniatures of what they will become. Being born in mid winter has its obvious problems, and succumbing to the elements is a definite possibility, but there are advantage, too. Nearly two months of nursing and sleeping allows the cubs to grow big enough to be able to travel with mama bear when she wakes.

Yes, it's a long time until spring in the northland (and we don't need a sleeping groundhog to tell us that), but the birth of baby black bears at this time of year is a move in the warming direction.

WINTER WILD FLOWER SEEDS

FTER A COLDER THAN NORMAL December and January, we
ended these months in an upswing. Thanks to a brisk south
wind, the forecast of mid-twenties on January 31 became a
temperature in the low forties. It waited until the last day, but the
January thaw did happen. December and January combined for an
average temperature of 5.2 degrees. This much below the normal
11.2 degrees defined the coldest December-January combination in
the last twenty-five years (since 1983-1984).

Early February saw a warm spell along with lengthening
days. Many of us started to think of spring. Whether it is looking at
seed catalogs, or sports equipment or vacation plans, we begin
preparation for warmer times. We still have plenty of winter to go,
the mild weather has moved on and we are dealing with more of a
normal February again. But it doesn't hurt to plan ahead.

Plants that survive our winter have perfected this preparation. Way back last summer and fall they packaged their floral plans
for the coming warmer times. We see them each day in the seeds so
clearly visible now in winter. When we look out over a field or
swamp in winter, we see the past and the future. In the fields, meadows, roadsides, and swamps, we find what looks like dead, dried
sticks reaching above the snowpack. Upon closer examination, we
can recognize goldenrods, asters, thistles, milkweeds, and cattails
from late last summer. Back then, they filled this scene with yellows,
whites, purples, and reds. Such colors attracted our attention, but
also that of insects. Six-leg visitors carried off pollen in exchange for
nectar and in doing so, pollinated other plants, assuring fertilization.
And tiny seeds formed as the flowers faded in the frost.

Coping with winter in their own way, many of these plants
stayed alive underground though their stems died. High on these
stems, however, the hardy seeds live. Exposed to cold conditions,
the seeds take advantage of the situation. Many appear fluffy, almost like feathers. This material allows the seeds to drift off in
breezes, so common in open country, and the seeds get dispersed.

In the coming warmth, some will take root. Most do not, of course, but a few will find the right conditions to germinate while the parent plant lives on.

Two of the most obvious ones now are goldenrods in the fields and cattails of the wetlands. Both produce numerous fluffy seeds that slowly spread out in winter winds. Milkweeds and thistles are a couple of the best at sailing the wind. With large "parachutes" to catch the wind, these plants typically lose their seeds by mid winter. Going by a swamp now will reveal lots of brown cattail seed clumps waiting to let go and along roadsides we'll see the same on goldenrods. Mid winter, yes, but plants, too, are preparing for the coming spring and summer.

FOXES MARKING TERRITORY

E ARLY FEBRUARY IS when we note a couple of phenomena. The days are getting longer. Soon we will experience ten hours of daylight for the first time in more than three months. And, according to the calendar, we are right in the middle between the winter solstice and the vernal equinox. Our snow cover has been around usually for about seventy to eighty days by this time. No doubt, we will have plenty more subzero mornings too.

Besides being cold, February also gives us less snowfall than other winter months. The month is typically very dry. Still, thanks to the snowfalls of the previous month, we usually go through these weeks with a thick snowpack. Also during February, we see a melting-freezing fluctuation, and the snow may vary from being dry to wet to crusty.

The snow cover tells stories of critters that wintered here and are now more active in the longer, warmer days. I find coatings of new snow (and even the old snow during this month) a great medium for recording the happenings of our mammalian neighbors. The increased amount of sunlight has made some more active, and the milder temperature cause some of the sleepers (not the hibernators) to wake for some winter wandering.

During my treks through woods and fields, I find signs and trails of deer, foxes, coyotes, squirrels, mice, porcupines, rabbits, hare, shrew, weasels (ermine), pine martens, and fishers, with occasional movements from raccoons and skunks.

Following their routes is always interesting. I've found the stories of the foxes' intent in the last few weeks. As we ended January, they spoke of hunger when the tracks in the field revealed diggings in the snow in an attempt to get subniveal field mice. Tracks ranged far and, in a couple of cases, the foxes themselves were seen hunting in the daytime. Hunger kept them looking. Now, in February, their tracks and signs tell another story.

Many of their straight-line trails lead to small clumps, bushes, or trees where they stopped to sprinkle their urine. This "yellow snow" we can see , but it's just as clear to the foxes' keen sense of smell. The message is obvious, one fox is telling another that this region has already been taken for a home territory and is no longer available, and no trespassing.

Routes are regularly patrolled and remarked when needed. Fresh urine serves to notify others of continued residency. Within the home territory, the mated pair selects a denning site and will settle down to give birth later in the spring after a gestation of about seven weeks.

Some animals claim territory possession by songs, others by drumming or tree scraping. Foxes use their showy, smelly urine on the snow to let others know of a home site during these winter days.

INSECTS ON THE SNOW

THE RECENT SNOWS AND COLD have given us a taste of the late winter and with an ample snowpack and temperatures in the chilly range, we might think that one group of animals we are not likely to see is insects. But in the right conditions, we not only see snow bugs now, but some kinds are quite active, and we may frequently see them.

These conditions are common during many days in February. If the temperature reaches the mid to upper twenties, these insects can and do appear on the snow. Calm and cloudy days are the best, but some emerge on clear days and even during light snowfalls. Bugs on the snow can be of several kinds, with a few spiders as well. The most abundant ones are also the smallest. If the day warms to the thirties, the wet snow may suddenly look filled with pepper, but these little black specks jump around. Though minute, these insects move fast and frequently with the use of a tail-like appendage that sends them hopping about, hence the common name "springtails." Scarcely a tenth of an inch long, they gather on the late winter snow in numbers that are often uncountable. They are taking advantage of the warm temperature to feed and mate. Too cold or too warm sends them back down into their subnivean world.

Near open water of a stream or river, the first caddisflies and stoneflies may leave the wet home of their youth. Adults have long wings and long antennae. Most are dark colored on the snow. Since last summer, their lives were spent as aquatic larva in these same waters.

A few spiders, such as wolf spiders and dwarf spiders, may be seen scampering over the snow now too. During the coldest times, they take shelter beneath the snowpack, but with days in the twenties or thirties, they climb over the surface, apparently in search of a meal or another place to live.

But the most commonly seen snow insects at this time are a few kinds of flies. Three quarter-inch insects find the February temperatures and snow surface just right. Unlike most insects, these three unusual flies reach maturity in winter. One has wings and will sometimes fly, but the others are wingless. Winged and looking something like a mosquito are the winter crane flies. Besides the superfluous resemblance to the mosquito, they do not bite. Though able to fly, they are usually seen sitting on the snow and take to the air only when frightened or swarming. The other two kinds of winter flies are without wings. Each is dark and they tend walk or hop over the snow.

The snow scorpion-fly has a large head with antennae and a beaked mouth. It is more likely to hop on the surface than the similar wingless crane fly. This last crane fly has a small head, short antennae and usually is seen walking on the snow. This insect is widespread and though most abundant in February, it can be seen throughout much of the winter. All of these flies are mature now and if meet another of their kind, they will not hesitate to mate with it right on the snow's surface.

Many a cross-country skier has seen some of these snow insects at this time and wondered what they are and why they are here, another example of insect adaptation.

GOSHAWKS

A S FEBRUARY MOVES along towards March, we experience a blending of mid and late winter. Movements of the next season are becoming more noticeable. Longer daylight — soon we will have eleven hours — will trigger changes. Chickadees will sing their territorial "feebee" songs, woodpeckers drum on tree trunks as they speak of territory, and crow flocks get larger and louder during these days. In the yard, local squirrels and rabbits begin early mating behavior.

These signs are mixed with the reality of winter still with us. Snow depths of two or more feet are common in the northland. Travel and food finding can be hard. Subzero temperatures are not yet a thing of the past. For many critters the last days of winter can be the hardest to survive of the whole season.

Though feeding may be difficult for many, predators can have the hardest time in these conditions. This may be best seen in the world of the raptors. Owls that have wintered with us may struggle finding nocturnal mammal meals in this snow depth. And during these late winter days they may be joined by owls from further north, making competition greater. Late February and March are the best times to view the great gray owls and hawk owls as they move south for some hungry hunting.

This may also be a time to see goshawks. Nearly two feet long with a wingspan of three feet, this northern hawk is an impressive bird. Adults are a bluish-gray above, light below with many gray bars on the white feathers, and a white line above the red eye that gives a definite identification. Black bands on a long tail are also a key characteristic as well.

Young are nearly as big, but are brown with streaked undersides. As is true with many hawks, females are larger than males.

Goshawks nest in remote coniferous forests of the north country. Their range may extend throughout much of North America. Each fall as the chill of October and November moves in, goshawks fly south over Duluth's Hawk Ridge. Though many go by, some winter here and are regularly seen on local Christmas bird counts. All through the cold season, these fast-flying hawks remain in or near the nearby forests where they feed on a variety of mammals and birds. This diet may include hares, squirrels, grouse, jays, and, during hungry times, any smaller songbirds that can be snared. Even though their name means "goose hawk," those particular water birds are not likely to be caught at any time. Goshawks usually pursue prey in flight, but they have been known to run on the forest floor and through the snow in pursuit of meals. Occasionally, they will give their "*kak, kak, kak*" call as they survey their home woods.

At this time in February, we may be able to get some great views of these large woodland hunters as they perch and fly in the roadsides and neighborhood forests. Like other predators, many of their hunting trips come up empty. They catch prey only about ten percent of the time. But the impending snow melt is sure to reveal more prey as the season advances and wanes.

CRITTERS DEALING
WITH DEEP SNOW

THE HEAVY SNOWFALLS OF THE last several weeks have given the northland landscape a thick and lasting snowpack. The two or more feet of snow covering the ground is much more than seen for some winters. Sidewalks, streets, and roads need to be opened for us to move about properly, but we also need to clear the roofs, something we may tend to forget. But the deeper snowpack also has advantages. With nature's blanket over the ground, most homeowners need not be concerned with frozen septic systems and water pipes.

We are not the only residents of the north country influenced by heavy snow. Up until the recent snows accumulated, the active wildlife in the region could pretty well go anywhere they wanted. With the snows, all that changed. Critters needed to adapt, and they did.

Larger animals like deer form trails through deep snow. They are able to pack down the route enough to make travel easier. For the next several weeks, they move on these "highways" as they go about their daily activities. This includes browsing tree branches. The additional snow has given the deer the height to sample the twigs of cedar, dogwood, and maple.

Smaller animals, like squirrels and hares, move about in sheltered areas of the woods. Squirrels in the trees do fine above the snow, but they need to come down for a meal. Travel here may be a bit hard, but when they can they will walk on the snow's surface or tunnel, as red squirrels often do. Snowshoe hares live up to their name as they scamper on top of the snow. Snow conditions vary greatly during the last half of winter, and after some thawing and freezing, the hares easily hop over the drifts. When cold and powdery, they have a harder time with their usual gait.

Deep soft snow makes it difficult to recognize animals by their tracks. With feet and legs sinking deeply and with almost never a clear footprint, track recognition can be a challenge. Anyone who has ever snowshoed on a soft snowpack can attest to the fact that this method of travel does have its limitations. Not able to move as well in soft snow, hares are more likely to sit still for long durations or travel on beaten down paths.

Mice, voles, and shrews are usually not seen when the snow cover gets beyond a foot. In relative comfort, they tunnel under the blanket and go about their daily activities in their subniveal world. Predators may pop in to their sanctuary for a visit and a meal. But for the most part, a snowy winter is better for them than not. This is true for the local ruffed grouse population too. Snow drifts are often chosen as their temporary home.

A snowstorm disrupts the lives of all of us. Sometimes it will be more difficult for northland critters, sometimes not. In the weeks of winter still ahead, we'll see how they cope with the changes in the present snow cover.

RED-OSIER DOGWOODS

LATE FEBRUARY IS WHEN we find ourselves looking toward the warmer days to come. Even if temperatures are cold and winter-like, we may look for signs that indicate a change on its way. And the signs are here! Some, like the loud flocks of crows, calling chickadees, or the pre-mating behavior of the squirrels in our yards are quite easy to note. But others force us to take a closer look.

Trees have stood out in the cold all winter and now respond to the lengthening days. Many trees absorb heat from the sun in their dark bark and radiate it out to melt the snow surrounding their trunks. As we exit this short month, the trees regularly show circles of snow-free space near the ground.

Higher up on the twigs, many buds are swelling larger, and a few begin to open. Best known of these is the pussy willow. This small tree has furry buds that emerge at this time. The hairyness of these buds and those of quaking aspen opening in a couple weeks are adaptations to this chilly late winter climate. Later in the spring, they develop into catkin flowers, but now they are fuzzy growths on the stem—a welcome sight for many cabin fever sufferers.

Not as well known, another tree that shows signs of the time, is the small red-osier dogwood. This shrub-like tree rarely reaches ten feet in height and would not even be noticed were it not for the bright red branches start taking on.

All winter this little tree of roadsides, woods edges, and wetlands dealt with the dark and cold days. Deer found the thin twigs fine meals. But now as the days get longer, the trees respond by taking on a bright red color. Indeed, trees on south-facing hillsides or exposed to the sun along waterways or streets stand out as being so bright red they catch the eye of many passersby.

It is a bit hard to see what this reddening does for the tree itself, even though it makes for another delightful sign of the season for us. Perhaps the red is an accumulation of a substance that deters herbivores from browsing on these edible branches and, therefore, allows the buds to form in the coming spring.

Whatever the reason for the red, it is beginning to light up the late winter. And it will continue to do so. As the days get longer and the branches are exposed to more sunlight, the trees get redder. With the spring foliage, the scarlet twigs of the red-osier dogwoods get masked by the green leaves. But for now, this small tree demands our attention and announces the changing seasons to come.

FLOCKS OF CROWS

B Y THE TIME WE GET TO MID FEBRUARY, daylight has lengthened to more than ten hours. The vernal equinox is still more than a month away and there's plenty of snow and cold, but the trend has begun — things are slowly becoming more spring-like.

Buds on some willows and aspens may start to open. A few red-osier dogwood branches are beginning their color phase that leads to their name. But there's more. Squirrels that came to the feeders all winter are now starting to notice each other, and they go through hierarchy behavior leading toward pair bonding and pre-mating.

In the world of birds, we notice more calls from local resident barred and great horned owls at nights, and maybe even the "beeping" of the tiny saw-whet owls too. In the mornings, we often hear the "fee-bee" calls of chickadees and the louder grunting sounds from nuthatches while woodpeckers drum more frequently.

But, for most of us, the most noticeable sign of the seasonal changes is with crows. These large black birds are familiar to all and are good examples of critters that have learned to live well with people. Flocks often spend the winter with us and do well in urban and suburban settings as well as rural sites. Some northland residents say that the numbers of crows staying here all winter is greater now than it used to be and growing.

Highly adaptable and intelligent, crows survive by maintaining a diverse diet. Where there's food, they and their bigger cousins, the ravens, will find it. Winter flocks at this time of February become more active and vocal. Within the group, pair bonding and mate selection is going on. Flocks fill up with the influx of individuals that spent the bulk of the cold season south of us. These travelers return and try to join with and fit into the population of crows that wintered here. The cawing of these meetings and squabbles often happens in the morning, making many northlanders not appreciate them.

Virtually every morning from mid February through much of March, we will hear these social gatherings. Eventually, they will

41

settle down to nest building. The flocks break up and families begin. Usually we are alerted to this by seeing crows flying with sticks and twigs in their beaks. The males do most of this cawing and carrying of sticks, but with this species, it is very hard to tell male from female.

FEBRUARY
DAILY CLIMATE INFORMATION FOR DULUTH, MINNESOTA

Normals Records

DAY	AVERAGE HIGH	AVERAGE LOW	RECORD HIGH	RECORD LOW	SUNRISE	SUNSET
1	20	2	49/1931	-33/1996	7:33	5:12
2	21	2	47/1991	-39/1996	7:32	5:13
3	21	3	44/2005*	-33/1923	7:31	5:15
4	21	3	52/1890	-29/1996*	7:29	5:17
5	21	3	45/1877	-33/1936	7:28	5:18
6	22	4	51/1925	-31/1936	7:27	5:20
7	22	4	55/1886	-30/1933	7:25	5:21
8	22	4	52/1991	-31/1933	7:24	5:23
9	22	4	46/1877	-36/1899	7:22	5:24
10	23	4	45/1977	-32/1885	7:21	5:26
11	23	5	43/1918	-32/1988	7:19	5:27
12	23	5	45/1976	-33/1875	7:18	5:29
13	23	5	47/1947	-29/1905	7:16	5:30
14	24	6	48/1882	-24/1970*	7:15	5:32
15	24	6	46/1931	-30/1936	7:13	5:33
16	24	6	52/2011	-30/1973	7:11	5:35
17	25	7	52/1981	-29/1936	7:10	5:36
18	25	7	53/1981	-25/1966	7:08	5:38
19	25	7	51/1930	-28/1966	7:06	5:39
20	26	7	54/1877	-21/1963	7:05	5:41
21	26	8	57/1877	-27/1963	7:03	5:43
22	27	9	52/1961	-27/1889	7:01	5:44
23	27	9	53/1958	-30/1889	6:59	5:45
24	27	9	56/1931	-28/1965	6:58	5:47
25	27	10	53/1976	-26/1990	6:56	5:48
26	28	10	58/1895	-22/1919	6:54	5:50
27	28	11	54/1896	-26/1879	6:52	5:51
28	28	11	53/1932*	-26/1962	6:51	5:52
29	29	11	55/2000	-19/1980	6:50	5:53

*Denotes latest of multiple years
Average Temperature for February: 15.1 F
Average Precipitation for February: 0.81 inches
Average Snowfall for February: 12.4 inches

MARCH

ARCH IS NAMED AFTER MARS (*Martius*), the Roman god of war. March was the first month of the year in the old Roman calendar.

BEBOOKWAADAAGAME GIIZIS:
The Crust on the Snow Moon

PHENOLOGICAL NAME:
The Month of Crusty Snow
The Month of Snowstorms
The Month of the Vernal Equinox

Mᴀʀᴄʜ ɪs ᴀʙᴏᴜᴛ ᴜɴsᴇᴛᴛʟᴇᴅ ᴡᴇᴀᴛʜᴇʀ. Longer days give mild temperatures, more humidity, and snow as March takes slow steps towards the equinox and spring. We see snow storms, ice, subzero chill, but also fifty degrees. It is the time of greatest snowpack, often with melting-freezing making it hard to walk.

March is all about awakening. Chipmunks early in the month are joined by raccoons, skunks, and bears later. Early migrants arrive. We excitedly await the first robins, grackles, juncos, and purple finches. The red-winged blackbirds arrive and sing "konk-a-lee" at the swamps at dawn, while woodcocks perform the "pneet" strut and "twittering" flight at dusk.

Rivers open and Canada geese and mallards, along with a few mergansers and goldeneyes, pause here. Maybe flocks of swans too with a nearby great blue heron. The first kestrel finds a roadside wire, while red-tailed hawks and harriers fly over and the killdeers call in melted fields.

Tiny snow fleas leap about and nearby trees respond to the longer days. Lengthening pussy willow buds join the fuzzy catkins of aspen and alders. March is the beginning of the sugar maple flow. By late month, trees produce sweet sap, and the silver maples are in bloom.

March is the time of microclimates. Sunlit southwest-facing walls and hillsides warm before other sites. House flies and jumping spiders find these spots while the first dandelions and crocuses bloom at the base.

Bare ground holds a growth of snow mold as the cover recedes. Honey bees, leafhoppers, ladybugs, and wolf spiders wander wherever bare ground occurs, and ants build on their solar-heated mounds.

March turns the corner from winter with a glimpse and a step towards the hectic pace of the coming spring.

MARCH HAPPENINGS: THE CRUSTY SNOW MONTH

What to look for:

EARLY MARCH
- red-tailed hawks
- ravens
- mating behavior of hares
- snow fleas
- stoneflies
- tree circles
- pussy willow and quaking aspen buds

MID MARCH
- canada geese
- mallards
- common and hooded mergansers
- purple finches
- mourning doves singing
- raccoons and skunks
- first chipmunk
- snow melting on ant hills
- jumping spiders on sunlit walls
- sap flow begins
- dandelions and crocuses blooming on sunlit sites

LATE MARCH
- great blue herons
- turndra swans
- robins
- red-winged blackbirds and grackles
- juncos
- yellow bills on starlings
- american kestrels and harriers
- killdeers
- woodcocks begin their display
- garter snakes begin waking
- mourning cloak butterflies waking
- alder catkins begin ripening
- silver maples begin blooming
- snow mold

TREE TWIGS OF MARCH

ARLY MARCH IS A REMARKABLE TIME in the northland. We are
still in winter, but the rapidly lengthening days give us views
of what is to come. But early March can be wintery as well.
Just last year, during the first week, we dipped far below zero degrees (some reports in northern Minnesota were of minus thirty!)
and in March of 2007, we shut down as a blizzard of twenty inches
of snow raged.

Such returns to the previous seasons happen throughout the
year, and they are normal. But the longer daytime and persistent
sunshine will win the battle, and by late in the month, the new season will prevail. A few migrants gather in our yards. Maple tree sap
flows. And some dandelions and crocuses bloom in sunlit sites as
well. But early in the month, many winter-weary northlanders seek
signs of impending change.

The best places to see spring at this time is to look to the
trees. We see tree circles (melted spaces around the base of the trees)
even though it is way too early for leaves. Buds and stems that wintered out in the open also respond to the longer light. Several kinds
of trees react to the sunlight. The white (paper) birch in late winter
is different from early in the season. The branch tips, especially on
the top of the trees, take on a burgundy color. Were the tree alone,
we maybe would not notice this hue, but when grouped, the colors
do appear well. Once we see this tint, we see that birches are not
alone. Alders abound in the north country, and a passerby can detect a purplish color change. The small willows of the roadsides and
wetlands hold twigs of red while those of the larger black and weeping willows turn bright yellow. Maybe the brightest colored twigs
now come from one of the smallest trees, the red-osier dogwoods.
Living up to its name, the whole tree is now a bright red.

But what is most sought now is another small willow, the
pussy willow. These little trees go a step further by opening furry
looking buds. Chosen by many as a sign of spring and collected as
a remedy for cabin fever during March, these buds usually open in

late February in response to a mild spell, but by the first days of March they abound.

I find another budding of note at this time too. High in the quaking aspens, so common here, the buds of the male catkins open and show a furriness like that of the pussy willows. I see these aspen buds opening each year early in March without fail. Being on top of the trees, we may need to search hard to find them and we are less likely to gather them, but the quaking aspens will join these other trees starting in their growth towards the eagerly anticipated spring.

Red-Winged Blackbirds

S PRING HAS BEGUN AND THOUGH we may not always feel the weather we expect for this new season, we are seeing the longer days. For the first time since early September, we are experiencing about twelve and a half hours of light, and getting more each day. We've seen mild temperatures, snow melt, and rain, but still the chill can be here too.

The longer days trigger the bird movement we call migration and it is happening around us now. Along with the sunlight and warming to the fifties, we saw melting of the ice on the St. Louis River and within a day of these open sites, I saw Canada geese, trumpeter swans, common goldeneyes, mallards, common mergansers and hooded mergansers. Early northbound flights also have been recorded from bald eagles, golden eagles, rough-legged hawks and northern harriers. Besides the movement of these water birds and raptors, I've seen some songbirds also that did not winter with us.

During our quick warm up of mid March, I noted a lone purple finch at the feeder and a few juncos in the yard. Along the roads, I observed small flocks of robins as well. (Good numbers of robins wintered in the area this year, but I think the ones that I saw were migrants, one even attempted a song.) The return to colder temperatures and some snow and ice slowed other migrant songbirds for a while. Now as we bring this changing month to a close, spring migration is on the way again.

Each year the swamps take on a new form as the male red-winged blackbirds return and proclaim territorial homes with loud "konk-a-lee" songs. They are eager to come back and take a site where ample cattails and shrubs will allow for their nests. Female arrival time is still a few weeks away. Male songs are meant to tell other males that this section of the wetland has been claimed.

Another early migrant at this time is the common grackle. A dark bird about twelve inches long, they appear to be black until seen closer and in proper light an iridescence of purple and green shows up. Arriving in flocks, sometimes with red-winged blackbirds, (in the midst of the rain and ice on March 23, I saw such a flock) grackles are more likely to come to our yards and select larger trees, deciduous or coniferous, for their homes.

Flocks may even take over bird feeders on their arrival and with plenty of calls and songs, the feeding scene may get quite loud. Their call note is a "crack" sound while their song is a squeaky noise that has been compared to the opening of a creaky gate. They also gather insects and small aquatic invertebrates and so grackles may congregate also in wet areas, but only to get some meals.

Soon, as we proceed through April, we'll welcome back other songbirds such as bluebirds, phoebes, yellow-bellied sapsuckers, hermit thrushes and even the first warbler, but in late March, it is the blackbird and grackle that have returned to usher in these changes and let us know of other coming events.

JUMPING SPIDERS

MARCH IS BEST KNOWN AS A MONTH of snow, often coming in storms. Cold temperatures may linger, and some years can be very windy. What gets overlooked in this month is that March is also frequently a time of clear skies, and we may see the mercury climb to the fifties or maybe even sixty. But even without the warmth, the days are getting longer and often very bright.

March is the month of hot spots. South or west-facing hillsides or next to building walls quickly warm in the sunlight. During sunlit afternoon hours at such sites, we could see a thirty-degree difference between here and the nearby shade. Indeed, many northlanders who have been indoors all winter find these spots as delightful places to bask. And we are not alone. Here too is where we find many early spring things. The first crocus and dandelion will be in bloom in a couple of weeks, usually by the end of the month. Grasses start to green as the snow retreats here.

If we look at the wall of a building out in the sun on a clear March day, we'll see several early-rising critters wandering about as well. These usually represent those that hibernated or stayed active all winter. Earthworms rise and move across the warming soil towards moisture. Their telltale castings are scattered here. Ants that wintered beneath the ground in their colony now come to the surface in search for food. Also present are some recently awakened ladybugs or leafhoppers, both of which spent winter in the nearby lawns, meadows, fields, or buildings.

Higher on the wall, we'll see some house flies that survived the cold by crawling into cracks and going dormant. Like some other insects, they allow parts of their bodies to freeze, but are able to thaw out and move about with the warmth. Now they sit in the sun, raising their body temperature into action. Soon they warm enough to fly.

Here too, are the ever-present opportunists, the spiders, seeking these insects for a spring meal. Two kinds are most likely to be out hunting on these sunny sites. Lower, near the ground, are the brown-striped wolf spiders while higher on the wall are the black-white banded jumping spiders. (One of the most common ones on these March walls is called the zebra jumping spider.)

Wolf spiders remain alive and active under the snow all winter, but the jumpers hibernated in sheltered locations. Both now are hunting for prey. Neither builds a web, but instead, they use their good eyesight to find and stalk food. Wolf spiders run after insects to catch meals while jumping spiders perform spectacular leaps to secure theirs.

We usually pass by without noticing these early-season predator-prey dramas acted out in the sunlit hot spots of March. But for those willing to stop and take a close look, they'll see much happening here and a glimpse into the coming spring.

SQUIRRELS AT THE FEEDERS

THE LONGER DAYS WITH PLENTY of sunlight and milder temperatures have slowed the activity at my bird feeders. I still get about eight kinds of birds visiting each day, but those that come by seem to stay for a shorter time and the numbers are down from earlier days. The goldfinch flocks that were composed of about fifty just a couple of weeks ago have now dropped to about ten. And some days only a few purple finches arrive. Perhaps a snowstorm or cold will bring them back.

Despite fewer birds, the squirrels still show up hungry each morning. Most anyone who feeds birds will also have these bushy-tailed mammals coming uninvited as well. Many bird feeders consider squirrels as pests and use a variety of methods to get rid of them. Whether it is the type of feeder, food or location, I find almost nothing works to rid these arboreal rodents from the scene. I have long given up on stopping them, I just put out more sunflower seeds to satisfy everyone. Looking out on any of the mornings this month, I expect to see ten to fifteen squirrels.

By far the most common of our squirrels is the eastern gray squirrel, but it is not alone. Frequently, small energetic red squirrels come by too. And nearly every night, we are visited by the nocturnal flying squirrels. Seen rarely too is the more orange-brown fox squirrels. Variations occur and not all grays look the same. I have noticed in the last few years that among the ones with gray fur are those with a darker pelage: the black squirrels. Black squirrels are just a different phase of a gray squirrel. Correctly known as melanism, this color is genetic and ranges within local populations from rare to common. (The white or albino condition is nearly always rare.) As a recessive trait, melanistic squirrels will typically be outnumbered by the gray. It appears that about one-fourth to one-third of my yard's squirrels are ebony. This amount may be increasing each year.

Regardless of their colors, things change in late February in the squirrel world. Up until now, they seemed to be interested in only getting free meals each day. Now as they dine, they often pounce towards each other. Not always to fight for a tasty morsel, these movements often take them up trees, away from the food. Apparently what is happening is that the squirrels are determining an important hierarchy as they move into the spring mating season.

This pre-mating behavior of jockeying for position and rights to claim a mate will prepare them for the coming breeding time. With a gestation period of forty-four days and their first births to take place in April, gray squirrel mating season is soon to be happening.

It is hard to believe that in a few weeks, they will go from the feeding sites to their nests in nearby trees. And as late winter unfolds into the coming spring, they will take on a life much different from what we see here. And it is hard to believe that the fifteen squirrels I see in front of me now will disperse into the forests during warmer weather and I will see few in the seasons ahead. Whether gray or black, squirrels in the yard are influenced by the longer days and are now going through some big changes.

MAPLE SYRUP TIME

THE VERNAL EQUINOX, THE FIRST DAY of spring, has arrived! After the cold and dark season, light now prevails and will continue to do so for six more months. Along with these warmer, brighter and longer days now in this new season, we will see many changes. Early migrants are starting to arrive.

We might search the flower garden for the first crocus to be open, but we'll need to wait a bit more for this awakening experience. Though flowering time is not likely to begin until April, trees are showing some arboreal growths now. Catkins extend and develop pollen on the small alders and hazels. Buds are swelling on others. I especially see the enlarging buds on silver maples. But there's more happening with our maples at this time.

This is sap time. I have had some years when I began tapping maple trees as early as the first week of March, but by waiting until now, we get a better flow. Trees that have lowered their sap to the protection of the subterranean root sites for the winter, now respond to the warmer longer days by raising this life-giving liquid. Flowage takes place in thin vessels just inside the bark of the trees. If we want to collect this sweet substance, we need to drill in just a couple of inches. By putting in a tap with an attached collector, we can partake of these March maples. Though we can taste the sugar in sap, it is dilute (only about two to three percent) and much of the water needs to be boiled off to change sap to syrup. Boiling sap demands patience, persistence and just plain hard work, but most sugar-bushing folks agree that the finish product makes the whole project worth it.

Anyone wandering out among the maple groves in late March is sure to notice that we are not the only ones who enjoy this spring delight. Squirrels will even gnaw through bark to get to the sap. Birds may drink it. (An April migrant, the sapsucker, lives up to it name upon arriving in the northland forests.) Even butterflies find this dripping ooze. (Early spring sightings of mourning cloaks, hibernating butterflies, are often on maple sites.)

Mild afternoons followed by freezing nights tend to be best for the sap flow. They also provide good conditions for the formation of "sapcicles." Dripping sap from drilled holes or cracks in the trees will freeze to produce sweet tasting icicles. Such frozen delights are worth breaking off and sampling as we passed by. I have enriched many a March woods walk with this maple candy. Whether we collect it or not, the rising sap tells us that the trees, after standing out in the cold all winter, are ready for another spring with us, even though green leaves are still two months away.

ANGLEWINGS

THE RECENT WARM DAYS OF MID March caught most of us by surprise. Days with temperatures in the fifties during this time happen on other years and sixties has even appeared sporadically, but rarely do we have such temperatures to persist for as long as they did this year. Even the nights were milder than expected and our temperatures never dipped below freezing for more than a week. The snowpack measured at twenty-two inches on March 1 and fourteen inches on March 10 was reduced to virtually none by March 20. These conditions under clear skies brought about changes in us and earlier than normal awakenings in the world of nature.

Here in the yard, I noted more than three dozen crocuses in bloom. Starting out with the yellows on March 15, they were quickly followed by purple and white ones. Catkins on nearby alders showed change too. These long growths that hung from tree branches all winter now are extended and filled with ripe pollen. Bumping them sends out a cloud of this yellow dust. (Though not appearing much as blossoms, these ripe catkins are the first tree flowers of spring.) Usually this is a scene acted out in early April. Out under the bird feeders so filled with winter avians, I saw a newly risen chipmunk scampering about. And fluttering through this early vernal landscape was a mourning cloak butterfly.

Not very colorful, mourning cloaks get their name from the dark, nearly black, wings. Each of the four wings is lined with a margin of light or yellow color. The blackish shade contributes to the "mourning cloak" name, reminding early naturalists of a somber experience. Mourning cloaks belong to a group of butterflies known as anglewings, due to a notch on the edge of their forewings. Members of this group are unique in that they hibernate as adults. (When it comes to winter, butterflies run the gamut. Besides adult hibernators, some winter as eggs, others are larvae, a few go dormant in the chrysalis and even a couple will migrate.)

Hibernacula are cracks in wood, behind bark and even beneath house siding. Here they remain for the cold times, but are quick to respond when a mild day happens. The first sighting for me this year was March 18. Though much earlier than normal, usually early April, it was not the earliest I've seen (that record is March 7, 2000, on a seventy-degree day).

With not many flowers at this time, they seek meals from sap and any available pollen. Here they may be joined by a colorful cousin, the comma. Smaller, these little orange butterflies with black spots are also sleeping anglewings. Like mourning cloaks, they search for food but they also open wings to bask in spring sunlight. We usually see them in this pose. When disturbed, they quickly close their wings to show a dark bark-like appearance. Greatly camouflaged, they are hard to see when on trees. A close look reveals a small white curved mark on the wings under side. It is this arc that gives the comma butterfly its name.

If cold returns, they'll go into hiding again only to emerge and flutter about later. Yes, this mild time of March brought out many happenings earlier than normal and we don't even need to leave out yards to see them.

CANADA GEESE

B Y THE END OF MARCH, THE BIRD migration that started slowly about a month ago becomes more noticeable. The crows, bald eagles and red-tailed hawks that have been wandering north through the region during the last few weeks are now being joined by others. A few of these long-awaited migrants appearing in the last days of March or early April are purple finches and juncos coming to yard feeders. Perhaps an early robin or two will be seen in the neighborhood. And red-winged blackbirds soon will be call from the swamps.

Maybe the easiest migrants to see at this time are the large and loud Canada geese. With the extent of ice that still prevails in the northland, it may seem unlikely that some water birds, such as geese, will arrive. But seeking open sites, they are able to move in. First, a few hardy ones arrive, but within a couple of weeks, flocks become prominent. They join the wintering goldeneyes, mallards and mergansers and it seems that now as the ice begins to break up, nearly every open patch of water holds floating and diving birds. We think of Canada geese as being huge birds, considerably bigger than other water birds. Most are more than forty inches long with wingspans of about five feet. Though all show the characteristic black neck, white head markings and a gray-brown body, not all are this size. These geese are much more varied than might be expected. Out in the flocks of "normal" geese are scatterings of smaller ones. Some are only about twenty-five inches long with a wingspan of nearly four feet.

With the divergence, it comes as no surprise that they don't appear to be the same species. Recently, species designation has redefined with these birds. And what was once said to be just one kind is now considered to be several. In our area, this translates into two names for these geese. The large ones are still called Canada geese while the smaller ones now are known as cackling geese. This name has been used for years as a term for a species variation or subspecies, but now, a species.

Whatever we call them, geese rest here in our spring open waters for a while before moving on to nest later in the spring. Many will breed in local wetlands. Soon these early water birds will be joined by swans, cormorants, pelicans, grebes, herons and a variety of ducks as the April migration takes advantage of the thawing.

We all are now looking for many spring happenings. They vary from early flowers, tree buds, chipmunks, songbirds or fish runs. But in the case of the Canada gees, their size and sounds makes them hard to not see. Soon our daily commutes will be adorned by a V-shaped flock or two of these birds overhead.

DANDELIONS

ATER MORE THAN SIX MONTHS DURING which the dark hours of the day have outnumbered those of light, we now have about equal, but quickly moving towards the opposite. With the season of spring upon us, our days are longer and lighter. And they continue to get longer each day.

On these clear days of March, we see the effects of the spring sunlight. South and west -facing sites on hillsides or near buildings are the first to feel the warming rays. In these protected hot spots, the temperature may be twenty to thirty degrees warmer than a nearby shaded location. It is at these places that we truly see spring happening first. Here snow melt quickly reaches to the ground. Here we may see early-waking flies actively pursued by spiders in the sunlight. Here we see grass already turning green. And here we see the first dandelions of the season unfold.

This ubiquitous weed may not be sought after for most of the year, but now we may go out of our way to see these green leaves and yellow flowers that are soon to follow. Indeed, the first one is usually in bloom before the end of this snowy and cold month.

Dandelions get their name from the sharp lobes on the leaves. Such points reminded early naturalists of the teeth of a lion, hence the French name of "dente lion", the tooth of the lion. It is easy to see how the common English name of dandelion came from this term. Of European origin, this plant now grows just about everywhere in this country. The perennial and hardy plant survives winter largely because of a long tap root that extends many feet underground, far below the frost and chill of this cold season. Home owners who have tried to dig out this often unwanted weed can attest to the fact that the long root reaches beyond most of our ambitious excavation attempts.

Leaves, remaining all winter, allow this amazing plant to quickly respond to the first warmth and sunlight of early spring. These first dandelions are soon to be followed by others and by the middle of next month, hundreds of yellow blossoms may pop up from the edge of our yards. Flowers open during the day, but close with the darkness and chill of these early spring nights. Composed of many tiny flowers, dandelions are a type of composite. Flowers in this family are common in summer and fall, with the daisy, black-eyed Susan, goldenrods and asters, but few besides dandelions are in bloom in spring.

Dandelions get such a jump on spring and flowers so early that many times they have blossomed, been pollinated by the few insects now about and have gone on to form the fluffy ball of seeds before other spring flowers have even started to bloom. Most of these spring ephemerals don't emerge until the days of April or May.

No doubt, such a quick response that lasts throughout the growing season is another reason for this exotic plant's abundance. The first dandelion starting to bloom in the early spring days of March is often the last one to be in bloom in the fall, as frost and snow moves in during November.

MARCH
DAILY CLIMATE INFORMATION FOR DULUTH, MINNESOTA

Normal Records

DAY	AVERAGE HIGH	AVERAGE LOW	RECORD HIGH	RECORD LOW	SUNRISE	SUNSET
1	29	11	51/1883	-28/1962	6:49	5:54
2	29	12	54/1889	-29/1989	6:47	5:56
3	29	12	55/2000	-21/1982	6:45	5:57
4	30	13	56/2000	-18/1875	6:43	5:59
5	30	13	57/1878	-18/2003	6:41	6:00
6	30	14	60/1987	-16/1884	6:39	6:01
7	31	14	70/2000	-21/1955	6:37	6:02
8	31	14	56/1977	-17/1889	6/7:35	6/7:03
9	32	15	54/1911	-19/1982	6/7:34	6/7:04
10	32	15	54/1990*	-26/1948	6/7:32	6/7:06
11	32	16	60/1902	-24/1948	6/7:30	6/7:07
12	33	16	55/1903	-18/1880	6/7:28	6/7:09
13	33	16	57/2012*	-14/1895	6/7:26	6/7:10
14	33	17	68/2012	-12/1906	6/7:24	6/7:12
15	34	17	60/2010	-11/1956*	7:22	7:13
16	34	18	60/2003	-17/1885	7:20	7:14
17	35	18	75/2012	-15/1941	7:18	7:16
18	35	18	73/2012	-14/1923	7:16	7:17
19	35	19	72/2012	-26/1875	7:14	7:19
20	36	19	62/2012	-21/1965	7:12	7:20
21	36	20	68/1910	-14/1885	7:10	7:21
22	37	20	72/1945	-14/1888	7:08	7:23
23	37	20	68/1939	-17/1974	7:06	7:24
24	38	21	70/2012	-21/1974	7:04	7:26
25	38	21	64/1925	-8/1955	7:02	7:27
26	39	22	72/2007	-19/1965	7:00	7:28
27	39	22	79/1946	-8/1982	6:58	7:30
28	40	22	81/1946	-14/1923	6:56	7:31
29	40	23	63/1963	-9/1969	6:54	7:32
30	40	23	67/1918	-12/1923	6:52	7:34
31	41	24	71/2010	-6/1923	6:50	7:35

* Denotes latest of multiple years
Average Temperature for March: 25.9 F
Average Precipitation for March: 1.49 inches
Average Snowfall for March: 13.2 inches

APRIL

A PRIL GETS ITS NAME FROM THE LATIN word "aperire" meaning "to open". April is a time when many buds and flowers will open. A second etymology is that April is named after Aphros, the Greek name for Venus. It was formerly the second month in the old Roman calendar than had ten months.

ISKIGAMIZIGE GIIZIS
The Sugar Moon

PHENOLOGICAL NAMES:
The Thawing Month
The Month of Grass Fires
The Month of Spring Showers
The Month of Maple Syrup

APRIL IS THE THAWING MONTH. It has snow and thunder showers, chilly nights and mild days, freezing and thawing, puddles and fire hazards. Daylight stretches to fourteen hours with warming temperatures causing the ice to surrender. Rivers open early in the month, joined by ponds at mid month and lakes at the end.

Frogs celebrating their wake up, and the songs of spring peepers, wood frogs, and chorus frogs resonate from wetlands that held a snowpack only a couple of weeks ago. The newly aroused bumble bee queen flies low over the recently melted fields as she hunts a nest site. The first wood ticks show up in these same fields, mourning cloak butterflies feed on dripping sap, the green darner dragonflies arrive, and fairy shrimp appear in vernal ponds.

April is about dozens of kinds of waterfowl in the newly open aquatic sites, herons and yellowlegs on the shore, and red-winged blackbirds calling from the cattails. The phoebes return, tree swallows and robins find their ways back to our yards, while yellow-rumped warblers, fox sparrows, and hermit thrushes revive singing in the woods. We witness the departure of redpolls and Bohemian waxwings. Grouse drum, woodcocks "pneet," and snipe winnow in the pre-dawn with calls of owls and the flight of sleepy bats at dusk.

April sees the early nesting hawks and owls watching the baby squirrels and rabbits. Beavers and muskrats seeing life above the ice for the first time in months, while bears and woodchucks step out into the sunlight.

Grass greens in the lawns, and mosses and wild leek providing green in the woods. Hepatica begins the forest flora show with bloodroot and spring beauty right behind. Alder and hazel catkins lengthen while those of pussy willow and aspen mature. Syrup from sugar maples flows and blossoms from silver and red maples open.

April sees a return to spring sports, lawn mowing, and garden planting. And we enjoy a winter-weary spring break. April is the reluctant surrender of snow and ice in early month becoming a vernal fling by the end.

APRIL HAPPENINGS: THE THAWING MONTH

What to look for:

EARLY APRIL
- grouse drumming
- junco flocks arriving
- great blue herons
- tundra swans and white pelicans
- turkey vultures and harriers
- waking woodchucks
- ripe catkins of alders
- silver maple flowers

MID APRIL
- song, fox and white-throated sparrows
- yellow-rumped warblers and phoebes
- hermit thrushes and bluebirds
- variety of ducks in wetlands
- ruffed grouse, snipes, woodcocks and yellowlegs
- moving garter snakes
- calls from chorus and wood frogs
- anglewing butterflies
- wolf spiders among the dead grasses
- first hepatica in bloom
- last redpolls at feeders

LATE APRIL
- loons in the newly-open lakes
- tree swallows, ruby-crowned kinglets and winter wrens
- bitterns call from swamps
- first baby rabbits and frog eggs
- spring peepers and leopard frogs
- wood ticks
- bumble bees
- first dragonfly (migrant green darners)
- wild leek in the woods
- bloodroot, spring beauty and marsh marigold begin to bloom
- red maples in bloom
- lawn grass greening

WATERFOWL IN RIVERS AND LAKES

ACH DAY OF THIS FASCINATING MONTH gives us something new to see. Warmer temperatures along with longer days bring more migrants from the south. Flocks of robins are in the area now, and they are being joined by their cousins, the bluebirds. Juncos arrive in groups that we frequently see in our yards and along roadsides. On utility wires, we might see the newly returned kestrel while another raptor, the harrier, hunts from the wing. Meanwhile, the larger turkey vultures seek carrion meals.

New migrants can be seen in the wetlands as well. River ice is quicker to break up than that in the abundant lakes of the northland. What was a complete ice-covered corridor just two weeks ago is now a free-flowing channel that brings in more migrants. Water birds are quick to take advantage of these sites, and they trickle in during these days and nights. A few stayed in the open waters of Lake Superior and remained here for the whole winter. Most abundant of these wintering ducks are the mallards and goleneyes.

Canada geese came loudly onto the scene during March. By the end of the month, these species were joined by common mergansers, hooded mergansers and the first flock of tundra and trumpeter swans. Now in late April with more open space, the diversity of water birds continues. The small brown pied-billed grebe along with large dark cormorants make their way here, too. And more ducks arrive.

In the shallows are wood ducks, blue-winged teal, and shovelers, while diving ducks such as buffleheads, ring-necked ducks, and scaup can be found far out from shore. Not all birds of the waterways are swimmers. Along the edges, we might see wading birds such as the tall great blue herons and the small sandpipers and killdeer.

Later this month as some of the swamps and smaller lakes open, the show continues. The strange coots appear in the swamps. Here too, we may find the snipe and its cousin, the woodcock. Area lakes may hold flocks of white pelicans and by the end of the month the first loon will be seen and heard. Usually by the time April is ready to exit, so is most of the ice. The lakes are still cold, but plenty of critters can be seen here.

Forests are shedding their snowpack, and frozen ground thaws as well and the next migrants of spring are showing up. Soon woods birds will be flitting by in their usual large numbers.

April is when we note the break up of ice and water birds that take advantage of this scene. Most are resting to move on later for a nesting site—some in the region, others far to the north. It's best if we can watch them without causing them much of a disturbance.

RETURN OF THE PHOEBES

B Y MID APRIL, DAYLIGHT HAS LENGTHENED to about thirteen and a half hours. And, despite the fickleness of spring weather, days of warm temperatures will emerge from the wind, rain, and snow. Such days bring on a huge vernal wake up. Mid April is when the ponds formed by the melt of the winter's snowpack hold calling frogs.

These amorous amphibians recently woke from hibernation go about the business of the next generation. Others just got up from the winter dormancy seek homes as well. Queen bumble bees fly over the lawns searching for egg-laying sites. In the yards and gardens, we see the grass greening almost as we watch and a few flowers are opening.

This is also the time when we see more songbirds arriving on their northward trek. A few, such as grackles, red-winged blackbirds, robins, and juncos, already came back during the cooler days of March, but most of the migrants of the previous month were raptors (hawks, eagles) and water birds (geese, ducks). Now we are seeing the next batch of migrant songbirds in the region.

Longer days also bring on the hatching and emerging of various insects. These "bugs" of April are small and, except for a few of the more annoying ones, we hardly notice them. But birds do. Many songbirds specialize in feeding on insects.

April migrants include hermit thrushes, bluebirds, winter wrens, tree swallows, flickers, sparrows, and the first warblers—the yellow-rumped warblers. We'll need to wait for a couple of weeks to see the really big numbers of songbirds migrate through the region, but these early ones will keep us looking for more. And there is one that often comes right to us—the phoebe.

Belonging to a group of birds called flycatchers, phoebes are small, about six inches, gray and quite nondescript—pretty much a little gray bird. Were it not for its frequent nesting on our porches, garages, and barns, we would not likely be aware of them at all. But they find our buildings and with mud, often mixed with moss, they place a nest under the protection of a man-made roof. Other sites sometimes chosen for nests include dog houses and beneath bridges.

Here they get protection from weather and most predators while feeding on the insects attracted to such locations. Birds return early to stake out a home territory and quickly go about building a nest. Pausing from these duties, they snack on spring bugs and sing their two-syllable name-sake song. Males repeat a harsh emphatic "fee-bee" song, accentuated on the beginning note. Both sexes give a chip call if we get too close to their home.

By beginning their nesting already in April, phoebes are able to fledge young by June and have a second brood in summer. These families devour many insects that also live near our houses. With their pleasant song and an insect diet, many homeowners see the return of a resident phoebe as a delight of mid April each year.

TRIO OF FROGS WAKING
AND SINGING

MID-APRIL MEANS SPRING is in full gear. Many migrating water birds now rest in the wetlands. In the woods, early thrushes are arriving, while bluebirds, tree swallows, and sapsuckers join robins in our yards and parks. Also, on the forest floor, the first spring wildflower, the hepatica, has begun to bloom, while nearby, the leaves of wild leek (onion) peak through the leafy carpet.

Ice is melting rapidly from the smaller ponds and swamps and, in its absence, the frogs appear. Despite the cold water, newly awakened frogs go to these smaller bodies of water and prepare for the new season. In the northland, it is a trio of frogs that sings of the arrival of spring each April. The two- to three-inch wood frog is accompanied by a couple of tiny frogs—spring peepers and chorus frogs—and are the first ones to call.

These last two are each only about one inch long. All three of the early risers have survived the cold by going beneath leaves of the forest floor or grasses in nearby fields. (Despite what we are often told, they do not go under water for winter.) With little more protection than this, they allow parts of their bodies to freeze, but they thaw out quickly during these warming days. Remarkably, the cold seems not to bothered them now as they move into their next phase.

In the world of frogs, the males call to get the attention of the mostly silent females. Once she comes into his territory, mating will occur. The eggs, often appearing like balls of clear jelly, soon follow. In our region, frogs are not very diverse. We have only seven kinds of frogs and one kind of toad living here. Collectively this group is called anura.

Males of each of these eight species sing a song quite different from the other species. Also they don't sing at the same times. Specific females will respond only to similar males. We have three kinds that perform early in spring, three more in mid season and two that will linger into summer.

The three early ones are easy to discern. Wood frogs are gray-brown to reddish-brown with a black patch behind their eyes. Spring peepers are light-brown with a dark "X" on the back. Chorus frogs are brown with dark stripes—our only striped frog.

They are equally as varied when heard. Wood frogs produce a "gluck, gluck" song, often compared to a group of ducks or chickens. Spring peepers live up to their names and give a loud single-syllable peeping song. Chorus frogs make a series of clicking sounds said to be similar to the noise made by slowly running our thumb over the teeth of a comb or a pen on the spiral of a notebook.

All of these will sing during April days, mostly in the late afternoons or evenings. They are quiet in the early mornings. Wood frogs, probably the most widespread and loudest of the three, are the first to stop. Usually by the end of the month their breeding is completed. A deep freeze of a recent winter killed many of our spring peepers, but they are returning and with chorus frogs, and they sing through much of May. Take advantage of a calm evening and visit a nearby pond to applaud the early show.

SNAKES WAKING IN THE SPRING

ID APRIL IS WAKE UP TIME for many northland wild things. Though most hibernating mammals are awake by this time, other critters are also starting to stir. Early butterflies, the anglewings and bumble bee queens begin to move about in search of a nesting site for this year's progeny.

Unlike these insects, when our local frogs wake up, they let us know with plenty of calling. Moving to the nearby vernal ponds, they proclaim breeding territories with a variety of guttural sounds.

Also waking now, but much quieter and less noticeable, are the snakes. Due to our latitude, the northland is not a region of many kinds of snakes. Only two species, the harmless garter and red-belly (sometimes called copper-belly) are common here. Occasionally, green snakes and ring-necked snakes may be seen as well.

After a winter spent in underground cracks and burrows (these sites, known as hibernacula, are used each year and so the snakes go through a type of migration each fall and spring as they go to and from these places), usually in the company of others of their kinds, the serpents slowly move out into the open. Though April days are much warmer than the winter, they can still be cool. Responding to this, the snakes of spring are often seen sitting in sunny sites, soaking up a bit of warmth. Being cold-blooded animals (ectotherms), garter snakes use environmental conditions to control their body temperatures. Such sunlit spots provide warmth for their bodies. Sitting on rocks is fine for them, but unfortunately, crawling out on a sun-warmed black-top road can be dangerous.

Once warmed up, they are able to go about their early spring activities. Though hungry after such a long winter fast, the garter snakes are more interested in finding a mate at this time. Using pheromones (sexually attractive chemicals), the larger females attract many suitors. Eventually, one male outlasts the others and mating takes place. Eggs form in her body later in the summer. Such eggs are not deposited anywhere, but hatch internally, and babies are given a live birth.

Garter snakes are the most common snake in the north country. Bodies may reach two feet (large ones are usually females), much larger than the red-belly snakes. Garter snakes also wear light colored stripes not seen on the red-bellies. Snakes will vary in darkness and other patterns, but nearly always have the tell-tale stripes. Spring and fall are the times that the local snakes are most active. Now, as they wake, bask and move about, we are likely to see them.

BUMBLE BEES SPRING FLIGHTS

B Y THIS TIME OF APRIL, the woodland wildflowers have begun to bloom as sunlight penetrates to the forest floor. Red maples are filled with small male or female blossoms. Open meadows and fields are greening as April showers help along this cause and slow the fire hazards.

Among the recently-waking animals, frogs call for mates from ponds and chipmunks scamper through the yards in never-ending quests for food. Hibernating insects such as butterflies, ladybugs, and leafhoppers are commonly seen now too. With the snow gone in the woods and meadows, other insects that have slept through the cold months, like the bumble bees, are buzzing about. Large, hairy and up to one inch long, bumble bees are easy to detect as we walk in the backyard at this time of spring. Most are black and yellow, but some northland species have an orange color added to their abdomen. They also have surprisingly small wings and at first it appears that such structures could not help these large critters fly. But they fly well and the tell-tale buzzing sound is made by wing movement from which the bees get their name.

Bumble bees live in colonies throughout the summer, but as fall weather moves in, the entire group of workers (females) and drones (males) die—except for the queen. She goes off to a hidden site under leaves or a log and becomes dormant for the winter, but not before she has mated. Through the colder months, she holds sperm until waking in the spring. Already fertile, her early spring activities are different from many hibernating animals that look for a mate immediately after waking. Instead, her spring flights are directed in finding a location to begin a new colony. She does this by flying very low over the ground and often landing to check out possible sites for a home.

Flights and searches in the meadows often take her to tunnels and nests made by meadow voles (field mice) under last winter's snow. She appears to be in no hurry and is seeking the ideal place to begin her new family. Once the proper site is found, she proceeds to make it more to her liking by bringing in grasses, mosses and leaves. To this she adds pollen gathered from early blooming flowers and trees. Here she deposits her eggs.

The eggs hatch within four to five days and develop into sterile females that will take care of broods for the coming summer. It is not until late in the season that fertile males and females develop, shortly before the colony's breakup.

Adult bumble bees visit flowers to feed on pollen and nectar, much like their smaller cousins, the honey bees. Unlike these insects, bumble bees are native to North America and are more docile and slower to sting. Indeed, many a critter-watching person has touched them with no ill effect as the bees sat on flowers.

Clovers, orchids, jewelweeds, and milkweeds are just some of the plants that rely on these gentle giants to be pollinated. Later in summer, sunflowers and goldenrods catch their attention too. As you walk in the backyard this April, take time to watch the queen bumble bee's flight and search for a home.

WOODCOCKS

D ESPITE OCCASIONAL WET SNOWFALL and chilly mornings, the movement of April weather is warming. Days continue to get longer and, yes, spring is happening. Along with the snow melt, we see ponds and swamps opening now at mid month. Grass is greening, crocuses are blooming, and more migrants arrive each day.Out in the open areas of the St. Louis River, we can see Canada geese, tundra swans, mergansers, grebes and several kinds of ducks. Here too, we may glimpse a great blue heron and bald eagles. Red-winged blackbirds sing from the swamps, while robins, grackles, and juncos are right in our yards.

Many of the songbirds that return now are quick to announce their presence as they set up territories for the coming nesting season. Other birds proclaim ownership and courtship rituals in different ways. Ruffed grouse are on the logs for their springtime drumming and in the damp meadows and wetlands, the woodcocks strut their unusual display.

Each evening at about one-half hour after sunset and again in the predawn darkness, we might hear a weird "peent" call coming from these sites. The woodcock (also known as the timberdoodle) is an early returnee to our region, regularly arriving while snow, ice and frozen ground still prevail. These cold conditions do not stop their action. In the calm hours of dawn and dusk they perform. And I have been fortunate enough to see and hear them. Shielded by darkness, the male marches in a squatting pose, bobs his head up and down and gives a buzzing "peent" call. With so little light on the scene, I would not notice them at all were it not for this nasal noise. But the show continues.

Such a weird dance and sound seemingly would get the female's attention, but anyone who misses the first act of this courtship dance is likely to notice the second. After the male dances a while, he takes flight and spirals up a couple hundred feet, making only twittering wing sounds. At the peak of this flight, he sings liquid warbling songs and rapidly descends in a zigzag route, tweeting all the way down. Unless weather conditions dissuade the amorous male, he courts each morning and evening in spring until mating takes place. With the beginning of his family life, he retires to the wetlands and is seldom noticed for the rest of the season. Only if by chance we scare up one are we likely to see it. Not only do woodcocks live in places we usually do not visit, but also they are of a cryptic coloration. Their brown-colored body of eleven inches has a short banded tail. Dark patches mark the back, while the underside is a reddish-brown. The stout body has short legs with a long, three-inch bill. This bill is forced into the wet ground to feed on earthworms. Using a movable tip, they are able to grasp the worms. Such a flexible bill is rare in the bird world.

It would be easy to never know that these unusual birds live here were it not for the courtship display now being performed by woodcocks at dusk and dawn in our local wetlands and meadows.

RETURN OF THE GREEN DARNER DRAGONFLIES

B Y LATE APRIL, SPRING IN THE NORTHLAND has picked up in pace. The first flowers cautiously appear in the woodlands. Red maples blossom with small bright flowers. Grass, brown all winter, is now green. The bird migration that gave us plenty of water birds and raptors earlier, now shows early songbirds. Soon their diversity will add much to see and listen to in the forests. Frogs do their singing as well, and every vernal pond, permanent or temporary, now echoes with calls from these breeding amphibians. A little slower than the ponds, area lakes will shed their ice and open up for another season by the end of the month.

With all this happening, it may be easy to miss the insect's role in this spring scene. We often think of the coming flies and mosquitoes, but they usually make their first appearance in May. Others are here in April. Easiest to see of these are the butterflies that wake after being dormant throughout the cold season. Bearing names such as commas, questions marks, tortoise-shells, and mourning cloak, they emerge from cracks to bask in the spring sunlight and find oozing sap for meals as they flutter about the scene. And they are not alone.

Bumble bees and hornets also wake in April. Their sleep is one to prolong the colony. Only the queens survived from last summer's nests. Impregnated before going into hibernation, they now rise and seek homes for the next brood. Usually their spring flights are low above the ground as they search.

A few insects that migrated south for winter are returning now. Nearly everyone thinks of monarch butterflies as migrants. Their well-known flight is far to the south (central Mexico) and so a return now is too early. Typically, these large orange-black butterflies can be seen here by late May. Another migrant though is a regular arrival in late April, the green darner dragonfly.

The months of June and July are the best times to see these fast flying insects of the swamps and marshes, but this dragonfly is our first to appear. While other dragonflies winter as immature under water larva and mature to emerge in late May, the green darner goes a bit south of here during the cold time, coming back in late April.

Bodies of these large dragonflies are about three inches long. The extended thin abdomen (often called a tail) is attached to the thick thorax. (The name of darner comes from their body shape being superfluously like that of a darning needle.) The head has eyes that nearly wrap around it. Four clear wings extend sideways from the green thorax. In true dragonfly fashion, they dart forward, backwards and hover. And in their maneuvers, they are able to snatch insect prey. Males have blue abdomens. Females are more grayish-brown. When established, they select a territory along wetlands and soon place eggs here.

But for now, in late April, their appearance adds their delightful flights to our other sights of spring. These "mosquito hawks" (because they eat many of these insects) are always welcome residents.

HEPATICAS

URING LATE APRIL, WE SEE huge changes in the northland. Along with the fluctuating weather conditions during this month, the temperatures rise, and we experience the long-awaited thaw. The snow cover of the last one hundred fifty days is nearly gone. And the lakes follow the open ponds and swamps of early April by shedding their ice. For the first time in five months, these bodies of water are liquid again.

This is the beginning of a unique time in the woodlands. For a period of a few weeks, the woods is devoid of both snow cover on the ground and leafy cover overhead. During this brief time the sunlight penetrates to the forest floor. Plants that have been dormant in the frozen soil under the blanket of snow and leaf litter now perk up again. In true opportunistic fashion, they grab the available light and put forth rapid growth. Before this short time is over, these spring plants need to unfold their leaves and open blossoms to assure a livelihood. This is the beginning of the spring wildflower blooming time in the local woods.

Each year, I am one of many nature observers who go out to look at this colorful addition to the scene. Most grow only a few inches tall and hold petals of white and yellow. But after a long chilly winter, they are a delight to see. Before this show time is over, we will have seen violets, trilliums, trout-lilies, anemones, spring beauties, bloodroots, marsh marigolds, and dozens more. They spread over the woods often in a carpet that causes us to stop and take a closer look. With proper moisture and sunlight, we are in for quite a vernal treat.

Nearly always, they bloom according to a schedule with some quicker to open before others. By a month from now when the tree leaves are open, the shade-tolerant flowers take over. But each year begins with the same number one: hepatica. The strange name of this early blooming plant refers not to the flowers but to the three-lobed leaves that reminded some early naturalists of a three-part liver — hence hepatica or liverleaf.

85

Unlike most of the vernal flora, hepatica leaves remain out all winter. They turn purple during cold but revive to a green color in the warming weather. With the leaves already out, hepatica can quickly open the six petals. Colors vary from nearly white to pink to blue to purple. Like most of the flowers of the woods in spring, the plants are perennials. Once we've found a spot where they bloom, we can go back each spring to greet the old friends. I have never seen an April without them flowering and I have never seen another spring wild flower in bloom before the first hepatica. It is a true vernal pace setter.

Blooms will remain open for a couple of weeks as they attract attention of early-flying bees, but they fade in the growing shade of May. The pace is quick and the scene changes daily among the spring wild flowers. A diverse and delightful floral display greets us as we walk in the springtime woods. And it began with hepatica.

APRIL
DAILY CLIMATE INFORMATION FOR DULUTH, MINNESOTA

Normal Records

Day	Average High	Average Low	Record High	Record Low	Sunrise	Sunset
1	41	23	62/2010*	1/1975	6:48	7:37
2	42	23	65/1925	-4/1975	6:46	7:38
3	42	24	74/1929	-5/1954	6:44	7:40
4	43	24	69/1991	-5/1975	6:43	7:42
5	43	25	79/1991	2/1971	6:41	7:43
6	44	25	75/1900	2/1982*	6:39	7:44
7	45	25	73/1931	2/1936	6:37	7:45
8	45	26	74/1987	5/1974	6:35	7:46
9	46	26	80/1887	6/2007	6:33	7:48
10	46	27	84/1977	10/1962	6:31	7:49
11	47	27	78/1968	6/1940	6:29	7:50
12	47	28	73/1908	6/1950	6:27	7:52
13	48	28	74/1941	9/1950	6:25	7:53
14	48	28	82/1908	8/2013*	6:23	7:54
15	49	29	79/1913	11/1935	6:22	7:56
16	49	29	76/1958	4/1875	6:20	7:57
17	50	30	82/1987	8/1983	6:18	7:58
18	50	30	81/1915	12/1983	6:16	8:00
19	51	30	79/1923	14/1897	6:14	8:01
20	51	31	76/1987	11/2013	6:13	8:03
21	52	31	76/1990	18/1991	6:11	8:04
22	52	32	80/1990*	17/1909	6:09	8:05
23	53	32	80/1942	12/1909	6:07	8:07
24	53	32	82/1990	19/1956	6:06	8:08
25	54	33	81/1990	12/1972	6:04	8:09
26	55	33	79/1952	20/1996*	6:02	8:11
27	55	33	88/1952	18/1909	6:00	8:12
28	56	34	87/1952	14/1958	5:59	8:13
29	56	34	83/1965	13/1958	5:57	8:15
30	57	35	85/1952*	22/1966	5:56	8:16

*Denotes latest of multiple years
Average Temperature for April: 39.6 F
Average Precipitation for April: 2.43 inches
Average Snowfall for April: 6.9 inches

MAY

AY GETS ITS NAME from the Greek goddess "Maia," who was identified with the Roman goddess of "fertility" or "mother." A second school etymology is that May gets its name from the Latin word "maiores" meaning "elder" (major). May was the third month of the year in the old Roman calendar.

WAABIGWANI GIIZIS:
The Flower Moon

PHENOLOGICAL NAMES:
The Greening Month
The Month of Spring Wild Flowers
The Month of the Beginning of the Rainy Season

M AY SEES THE LAST OF THE SPRING snow flurries, and the snow that has covered our ground for such a long time is now gone. May is the beginning of our rainy season with showers and the ever-increasing thunder showers. It's a warming month: a few days in the eighties blend with frosty mornings. We see warm afternoons and lingering evenings. The month has lengthening days of early sunrises and late sunsets.

May is a month of change. What begins as a brown meadow ends with tall green grass. What begins as a woods of bare trees and dead leaves on the forest floor ends as a green shady forest, as the forest floor comes to life and dozens of spring wildflowers grow quickly to catch the sunlight while it is available. The anemone, spring beauty, bloodroot, and hepatica gracing the eye early in the month are replaced by Clintonia, trillium, columbine, and lady slippers at the end. Fern fiddleheads, morels, and scarlet-cup fungi appear in these same woods. Trees flower and roadsides light up with blossoms from plum, juneberry, pin cherry, choke cherry, apple, and lilac.

May has butterflies flitting to these early flowers and the queen bumble bee settles on a site to raise her colony. The songs of returning warblers, thrushes, wrens, sparrows, and tanagers greet our ears as they claim their real estate in the early morning and again at dusk. The new fawn just dropped lies motionless.

Ice goes out on northern lakes in time for the fishing opener. Ducks and loons nest on those same lakes. Nights grow loud with the calls from spring peepers, leopard frogs, and toads as they reproduce in the swamps and ponds.

Trees bare for months leaf out and grow at rates of one-half inch per day. Lawns need mowing and gardening revives. May is all about bird eggs, baby rabbits, caterpillars, wood ticks, mosquitoes, and black flies. Dragonflies emerge at the lake.

May is a month of huge changes that leads us into the heat and growth of summer. May is the greening month.

MAY HAPPENINGS: THE GREENING MONTH

What to Look For:

EARLY MAY
- arrival of ovenbirds and other warblers
- spring azure butterflies
- beginning of mosquito season
- blooming of wood anemone, wild strawberry, violets,
- trillium, trout-lilies, bellwort, and spring beauties
- marsh marigolds light up the wetlands
- elderberry and gooseberry leaves opening

MID MAY
- return of rose-breasted grosbeak and orioles,
- veery and wood thrush
- American toads call
- painted ladies and veined white butterflies
- morels, false morels
- fern fiddleheads
- blooming dutchman breeches, wild ginger,
- jack-in-the pulpits, toothwort, trailing arbutus
- wild plum and pin cherry
- leafing of lilac, willow, poplar, aspen

LATE MAY
- arrival of ruby-throated hummingbirds,
- diverse species of warblers,
- red-eyed vireos and scarlet tanagers
- gray tree frogs call
- dragonflies begin to emerge from water
- crickets begin calling
- first tiger swallowtails and skippers
- return of monarchs
- blooming columbines, baneberry, starflowers, clintonia,
- yellow and pink ladyslipper orchids
- juneberry and choke cherry blossoms
- apple blossoms and lilac
- the greening of the woods

FOREST FLORAL DISPLAY

THE WOODS OF EARLY MAY ARE truly amazing. Each day the wanderer here will find something new from the day before. Early warblers are darting through the branches and, in typical fashion, they keep moving. Thrushes and sparrows join the new migrants along with a few swallows and flycatchers. Wood frogs that called so loudly from the ponds in April are now silent, their breeding done for the year. They scatter into the forests while spring peepers and chorus frogs continue during May. Soon we'll start to hear the first gray tree frogs and American toads as well.

May is the greening month in the northern states. This is easily seen in our lawns and gardens, but it's happening in the woods too. Here the greening is from the bottom up. Mosses and wild leeks (wild onions) along with clubmosses and evergreens from last fall start it off. After these forest floor plants, shrubs and small trees are next to open leaves. The canopy overhead is the last to green, but now we see leaves opening on the small elderberry, raspberry, and gooseberry, with aspens starting the leafing of the taller trees.

Before the canopy leaves cover the ground with shade, a whole group of wildflowers quickly grow, open their blossoms, set seed and fade by month's end. With such a short growing time, it's hard to believe they reach the leaf and petal size they do. Hepatica is the first to open, mid to late April, followed by white bloodroots and pink spring beauties. Yellow carpets of marsh marigolds take over sunny parts of wetlands while wild strawberries open in fields. But most of the vernal flora display is on the forest floor where shade later in the month and all summer forces the opportunists an early start.

Here we soon see violets of several colors, yellow and white trout-lilies, and the strange looking jack-in-the-pulpits. Though lots of these early flowers are small, white trilliums fill the May world with large white blossoms, often in carpets.

The name trillium describes the number of petals, "tri" meaning three. Not only are the white petals in triplicate, but so are the sepals and leaves. Plants reach up to a foot tall, and the flowers may be three or more inches across. Besides the fact that trilliums open such a splendid bloom, they frequently grow in large numbers and hillsides of hundreds or more make us want the flowering season to last longer. After a week or two of such a show, the petals fade to a lavender color before dropping, a bit of an encore. Despite this massive flowering, they are gone and forgotten by summer. Only the observant searchers will note the red berries produced in late summer as being part of the mass flowering of May.

The May magic floral parade continues in the woods until shaded by the overhead leaves. By June, we will have seen at least another twenty kinds of flowers, including another trillium, the smaller and harder-to-see nodding trillium, that will come and go. And nature observers will continue to find a new show every day this month.

FALSE MORELS: THE FIRST FUNGUS OF SPRING

IN THE FIRST WEEK MAY, many of the spring wildflowers that were in bloom earlier this week are accompanied by nearby plants still not flowering, the shade-tolerant ones, but they will soon open their petals. A walk in these same woods in about ten days will reveal whites starflowers, wild lily-of-the-valley, and baneberry with yellow from early Cintonia (blue-bead lily). The forest floor is changing.

Among these vernal herbaceous plants, a plethora of fiddleheads from about a dozen kinds of ferns begin to emerge about the time the reddish leaves of maple saplings abound. As I looked over this lush spring community, I noticed a member of another sort as well, a distorted-looking brown growth balanced on a thick white stem. The whole thing was about three inches wide and as tall. A closer look revealed a false morel, the first new fungus to appear in spring.

By late summer and fall, fungi, especially mushrooms, are very common in the forest. Many go beyond this site. We also see them in yards and parks. Though May gives an abundance of plant growth, fungi are not common, but a few do appear in this season. With the foliage of May, I have occasionally found a bright red cup fungus. This adds a delightful color to the whites and yellows of the spring flowers. But probably the best known of these springtime fungi are the morel and false morel. Standing a few inches above the soil, they have light-colored stems that hold caps littered with holes and folds (morel has also been called sponge mushroom). They are also known as May mushrooms and pine-cone mushrooms, but most of us know this well-loved fungus, often collected for meals, as morels. (Morels have been selected as the state mushroom of Minnesota, a bit ironic since they reproduce differently and are not true mushrooms.)

Not as well known was the fungus I found this week, the false morel. A casual observer could confuse the two, but anyone seeing it closely will not mistake one for the other. (False morels should *not* be consumed.) Both have a light stem that holds a brown spongy cap, but the similarity ends here. The cap of the morel is attached where the stem ends, the false morel has a cap extending down over much of the stem. Morels are shaped more like a cone, while its cousin resembles largely undefined folds and is often darker.

Morels and false morels appear at this time of year on the soil among the trees. Recent rains (and snows), adding more moisture, increase their likelihood of being seen. Though morels are the sought ones, both are a delight to find in springtime, and they start off the fungus season that will last through the warmer days to come.

SPRING AZURES OF EARLY MAY

WHEN COOL DAYS OF LATE APRIL give us temperatures of ten to fifteen degrees below normal with several snow showers, the progress of spring can slow. With warm temperatures, things quickly get back to when we expect them to be.

The northward warbler movement has begun, and soon forest trees are holding dozens of these small flitting birds. The four kinds of frogs already calling and breeding in April are joined by two more in May—the gray tree frog and the American toad. Leafing out, begun on the forest floor moves up into the smaller trees and continues upward into the canopy. And the carpet of spring wild flowers continues to unfold throughout the month.

With warmer and longer days, we'll see new butterfly species, too. The anglewings (mourning cloaks, tortoise-shells, and commas) hibernate as adults and so are present and fully grown when the spring begins. Other butterflies spend the cold season in a variety of ways. Some survive as eggs. A few hatch and remain in the caterpillar stage. Others are in the chrysalis (cocoon) throughout winter. And, of course, a couple kinds migrate (monarchs are not the only ones).

Not the first butterfly, but the tiny spring azure is the earliest to emerge from its chrysalis. Each year, during the first two weeks of May, the tiny spring azure becomes an adult and shows up in our yards and gardens. These fluttering insects are only about one-half inch long with a wingspan of one inch. With plenty of ease, they could sit on our finger tips. Blue above and white below, they reveal this double pattern so common in butterflies where the color on the wing's surface is completely different from that beneath. The white below is filled with dark dots and arcs, but no bright orange as seen in some similar blue butterflies.

Mating and egg laying are about all that can happen in the short life of these diminutive butterflies. The adult stage will last only a week or two. After successfully laying eggs, adults will exit spring before most other butterflies enter. Egg hatching corresponds with leaf emergence. Caterpillars feed on the newly formed leaves of dogwood, cherry, and viburnum. Young of the blue family are often discovered by ants and taken home. Some are even cared for in the colony until a new chrysalis is formed.

The already delightful days of May will soon be made more so with the sighting of these small blue butterflies. They speak to us of many more kinds to come.

COLUMBINES

THE EARLIEST OF THE SPRING WILDFLOWERS take advantage of the long days of early May to do their blooming. Here on the sunlit forest floor they open their yellow, white, or purple petals and get the attention of spring bees. After a quick growth and short flowering time, they fade nearly as fast as they appeared. Such quick-living plants are often called ephemerals.

With the trees starting to fill out the canopy above, the next batch of wildflowers begins to show its petals in late May. These include plants more shade tolerant than the ephemerals, but also many grow at the woods' edge, wetlands or open sites in the forest. A walk now in the woods may reveal some of the earlier spring beauties. Bellworts and trilliums are still blooming, but plenty of new flowers are starting to open too.

On the forest floor starflowers and baneberries open their white blossoms while the strange looking green-and-purple jack-in-the-pulpit also blooms here. Nearby, along trails, open woods and rocky hillsides, columbines add their colorful blossoms as well. The plants stand up to two or more feet tall. At the end of the branches hang the red-and-yellow bell-like flowers. These five hollow petals have long spurs that extend beyond the base. Including the spur, these delightful flowers may be up to two inches long. Spurs and petal exteriors are red while the insides are yellow.

The spurs give columbine it name. The word means "dove," and the five spurs reminded some observers of a group of doves sitting in a circle. The scientific name of *Aquilegia* tells us that other naturalists have seen these spurs as talons of an eagle. The reddish spurs contain nectar, and this flower, named after two kinds of birds, is often visited by another, the hummingbird. The colors and shape of these flowers allow hummingbirds to reach in to sample the nectar. Bees also come to the columbine flowers, and they are responsible for the bulk of this plant's pollination.

Leaves can easily get overlooked with such showy flowers, but they are worth noting too. The lightly notched foliage of the columbine is similar to that of a related flower, the meadow-rue. Though they don't look the part, both the columbine and meadow-rue are in the family of a well-known yellow flower, the buttercup. Known as the crowfoot family, many members have deeply cut leaves that are said to resemble the toes of a bird.

When getting enough sunlight and moisture, columbines grow tall and bloom profusely. Their flowering season can often last into July. Visiting some of the northland rocky hillsides, especially those facing south, can get us some great views of these red-yellow columbines. Even some of the bare rocky cliffs sport a bouquet or two of these bright flowers. And they begin this blooming now in late May.

THE TOAD SEASON

ACH SPRING, USUALLY BETWEEN MAY 10 and May 20 (later in some chilly years), animals that normally stay away from water, come to the water in large numbers. And though they are silent for nearly all of the year, they become quite loud at this time. Mid May is the breeding season for the American toads.

Most of us see toads in yards and gardens where they appear in summer, usually alone, to feed on insects and spiders. Related to frogs, they differ in a couple of obvious ways. Toads have a much rougher and dryer skin. Their back is filled with bumps (often called warts). And their back legs are shorter than the back legs of frogs. Therefore, their ability to hop is much less. Being of dry skin, they do not go to water or want to be wet like their frog cousins. Normally, water is only something they drink, like other land animals.

However, when it comes to egg-laying, they need to return to their place of origin, the nearby ponds and swamps. Here they grew up and left in recent years. Breeding in the world of toads is quick and loud. Triggered by temperatures and length of day (and night), toads move in from the surrounding lands to local wetlands. The males call for the attention of the females and to establish a site or domain. We might expect such a dry and rough-looking critters to have a very deep "ribbit" or croaking type of voice, but quite the opposite is true. Toads sing a high-pitched trill that may go on at least thirty seconds, non-stop. With a breath or two, they call again. Once the breeding is serious and active, calls continue all day and night.

Anyone visiting a pond at this time will be surprised to see these land-loving toads so at home and swimming in the water. Aquatic courtship and mating continues around the clock for a few days, maybe three to five, and then, just that fast, it's over. Indeed, many of us are not even aware of this pond event until after it has passed. The adults disperse back to their terrestrial life again where they spend the summer feeding on insects and other small critters.

The product of their breeding can be seen along the edge of the wetlands in the next few days. Strings of jelly-covered eggs

101

stretch out there. Unlike frogs, toad eggs are in long strands while frogs produce eggs in ball-shaped masses of jelly.

Soon, tiny tadpoles appear. These dark critters stay close together through the coming weeks, often looking like dark splotches at the pond's shore.

Their growth is rapid throughout June and, by mid-July, we start to see the tiny toads coming onto land in large numbers. These fingernail-sized critters will get preyed on by many others, but enough survive to trill again next year at this time.

BIRD MIGRANTS OF MID-MAY

URING THE SECOND HALF OF MAY, the tree tops become more alive. The green leafing is now reaching the pinnacle. Large trees, the last ones to unfold leaves, now do so in abundance. The woods now wears a thick canopy and shade persists in these sites until next fall.

Here too is where we see the active newly arrived migrants. Though vireos, flycatchers, orioles, tanagers, and finches all make their appearance, the warblers dominate these May migrant birds.

About fifty kinds of these small birds can be found in the United States, twenty-six of which pass through the northland each spring. Some stay to nest, others keep moving. All seem to be hyper as they flit among the leafing branches. It is no coincidence that these little birds come here at the greening time. They are insect eaters, and an abundance of insect larvae (caterpillars) feed on these newly-formed leaves. Warm weather and rain brings in plenty of food for the warblers.

Warbler names often speak of their colors: yellow, yellowthroat, black-and-white, chestnut-sided, bay-breasted, golden-winged, orange-crowned, yellow-rumped, black-throated green, black-throated blue, blackpoll, and redstart. Some are named after places where they nest or where they were seen while migrating: Canada, Connecticut, Tennessee, Nashville, and Cape May. Others are named after trees where they were seen either here or in migration: pine, palm and magnolia. A couple are named after people: Wilson's and Blackburnian.

Mourning warblers get this name from a dark hood appearance. Waterthrushes look like the larger brown-spotted thrushes. Parula refers to its small size. Ovenbird is perhaps the strangest warbler name. This epithet comes from the bird's nesting in a hollowed chamber of a mound of leaves on the forest floor. We frequently hear them at this time as they loudly proclaim their "teacher-teacher-teacher-teacher" song. No wonder they are often called the "teacher bird."

103

Though the word "warbler" may mean song, most warblers are rather weak singers. A few, however, like the ovenbird, give diagnostic sounds. The blue-yellow parula sings up the scale. Yellowthroats give a "wichity-wichity-wichity" call from the damp grasslands. Black-and-white warblers repeat a simple "we-see" whistle many times. Yellow warblers sing "sweet-sweet-sweet, I am so sweet" while the chestnut-sided varies this call as "sweet-sweet-sweet, switch you" from small trees. Deep within the woods, we hear the "zee-zee-zee-zoo-zee" of the black-throated green warblers.

A good pair of binoculars and patience is needed to search for these small fast-moving birds. But with persistence, we can see twenty or more in one day now. Whether we see that many or few, witnessing the warbler migration of late May is one of the annual phenomenon we are fortunate to see in the northland. Migration flights often happen at night and so we may wake to several new ones in our yards each day.

BALTIMORE ORIOLES

THESE DAYS OF LATE MAY are filled with activity. The spring that has been greening all through this month now seems to be mostly complete and even trees reluctant to open leaves are growing their foliage. Three completely unrelated trees are consistently the last to fulfill this task: black ash of the swamps and staghorn sumacs of the roadsides and bigtooth aspen. With maples, oaks, and basswoods all fully foliated, the woods has become dark-green and shady.

Changes here are noticeable. The forest floor flora of early May is quickly being replaced by more shade-tolerant ones. Migrant songbirds returning all through this month are still on the move, but now are harder to see as they flit among the leafy canopy. Until now, we could search the mostly open branches to see these active avian songsters. With birds hidden in the leaves, we now need to rely mainly on their songs to locate them.

Many of the returning migrants will remain with us for the duration of their breeding season. In the world of songbirds, this means singing on the chosen territorial site where they will dwell. Usually, it is just the male who sings, and he isn't satisfied in proclaiming his ownership just once. No, he repeats it often.

Most of us can't recognize all the birds by their songs, but a few birds are loud and frequently near our house and yards. One of the best of these is the Baltimore oriole. These boldly colored black-and-orange birds are quick to sing upon returning to the northland, usually arriving about mid May. At that time their plumage makes them easy to see in the greening treetops. If we don't see them, we can definitely hear oriole vocals that sound like a series of rich whistles and calls, often the loudest one in the tree tops.

Even more delightful is the orioles' desires to come close to us as they visit our feeders. I have seen them interrupt their songs to come to two kinds of these feeding sites. Sliced oranges did the job of attracting these birds to where we scattered sunflower seeds all winter. (I'm not sure if it is the color of the oranges or the food that brings them in.) Others have seen orioles come to grape jelly on feeders too. I also watch them up close as they satisfy a sweet diet by sampling sugar water of the hummingbird feeder. The red on this feeder that attracts ruby-throated hummingbirds also can catch the eye of these showy Baltimore orioles. They seem to chatter much when alighting on this feeder.

Female orioles, though orange, are not as bright as males and lack the black head. Both are regularly in the yard in late May. Soon they will go off to construct a nest. Using grasses, hair, and string, they meticulously weave a bag that hangs from high branches of large trees (often willows and elms) where they raise a family. Loud songs continue at this time, fading with the months of summer. But what a treat of sight and sound the Baltimore orioles now are.

Yellow Ladyslipper Orchids

A
S MAY ENDS, WE LOOK OUT on a green landscape. Lawns, roadsides, and fields have quickly greened as well. And the forests have leafed out. Even the last trees, usually the large ones, have a new set of leaves. The woods is now shady.

Spring wildflowers that thrived just a couple of weeks ago as sunlight penetrated to the forest floor are now fading. These ephemerals took advantage of their short-lived opportunities. Some will have leaves lingering into the summer season. Others will drop leaves and disappear from view. By July, we will not even see that they bloomed here in May.

Their place is taken by more shade-tolerant plants. Starflower, corn-lily (clintonia, blue-bead lily), wild lily-of-the-valley, sarsaparilla, baneberry, and bunchberry will all bloom where the earlier bloodroots, spring beauties, and bellworts were. Soon proliferation of the flowering plants will be seen in the open roadsides and fields of June. But among those still in the woods are the ladyslipper orchids.

Many kinds of orchids can be found by the diligent searcher in the northland. Most are rather small and a good number are in swampy sites, hard to get to. But some, like the ladyslippers, are well worth the trip. These stand out as being large and colorful, yellow ladyslippers, pink ladyslippers (moccasin flowers), and showy ladyslippers (the state flower of Minnesota).

Pink ladyslippers tend to be in the acidic soils associated with bogs and pine forests. Showies, also of wetlands, bloom later in the season. Yellow ladyslippers are blooming in some of our area mixed forests in late May. We are fortunate to have such huge growths of these beautiful flowers along trails at some nearby state parks. Plants reach up to one and one-half feet tall and though not always in big populations, they are rarely alone. Stems are very green with several long leaves protruding. Pink ladyslippers differ greatly in this aspect by having their two large basal leaves near the ground, none on the stem (which is technically not a stem).

Above the leaves is the hollow oval-shaped yellow flower. Petals have fused to make this growth. Nearby are brownish petals, which are twisted or braided in appearance. This arrangement of yellow and brown makes for an interesting and beautiful plant that we will be able to view over the next couple of weeks from late May to mid June.

Ladyslipper orchids are a bit mysterious in their life cycle. They are perennials and are often many years old. Despite this age, they are fragile and frequently do not survive transplanting. Plants have a mycorrhizal association with soil fungi that can be easily disturbed and difficult to regrow. Late May is a great time to get out and see these yellow ladyslipper orchids, but do not pick them. Take only pictures though.

MAY
DAILY CLIMATE INFORMATION FOR DULUTH, MINNESOTA

Normal Records

Day	Average High	Average Low	Record High	Record Low	Sunrise	Sunset
1	57	36	86/1959	19/1966	5:54	8:18
2	58	37	86/1880	21/2002*	5:52	8:19
3	58	37	85/1952	16/1907	5:51	8:20
4	58	37	86/1980	23/1967	5:49	8:22
5	59	38	87/1918	19/1989	5:48	8:23
6	59	38	82/2000*	20/1989	5:46	8:24
7	60	38	88/1896	24/1907	5:45	8:25
8	60	38	87/1896	22/1966	5:43	8:27
9	60	39	88/1896	20/1966	5:42	8:28
10	61	39	86/2007*	23/1981	5:41	8:29
11	61	39	83/1991	23/1963*	5:39	8:31
12	61	40	84/1940	24/1946	5:38	8:32
13	62	40	86/1977	22/1997*	5:37	8:33
14	62	40	91/1932	27/1921	5:36	8:34
15	62	40	88/1931	26/2004	5:34	8:36
16	62	41	84/1962	20/1929	5:33	8:37
17	63	41	87/1972	26/1988	5:32	8:38
18	63	41	87/1998*	27/1915	5:31	8:39
19	63	42	87/2012	26/1929	5:30	8:41
20	64	42	88/2009	26/1986	5:29	8:42
21	64	42	88/1964	28/1971	5:28	8:43
22	64	42	90/1964	30/1917	5:27	8:44
23	64	43	84/1980	28/1917	5:26	8:45
24	65	43	84/1875	31/1949	5:25	8:46
25	65	43	86/2010	30/1992*	5:24	8:47
26	65	43	85/1978	28/1992	5:23	8:48
27	65	44	86/1969	31/2008*	5:22	8:50
28	66	44	91/1934	32/1965*	5:21	8:51
29	66	44	87/1986	29/1984	5:21	8:52
30	66	44	95/1939	29/1990	5:20	8:53
31	67	45	89/1925	29/1946	5:19	8:54

*Denotes latest of multiple years
Average Temperature for May: 51.4 F
Average Precipitation for May: 3.23 inches
Average Snowfall for May; 0.4 inches

JUNE

THERE ARE TWO ETYMOLOGIES FOR JUNE. The first is that June gets its name from the Roman goddess Juno. The second is that June gets its name from the Latin word "iuniores," meaning the "younger ones," following the month for "elders" in May. June was the fourth month of the year in the old Roman calendar that had ten months.

ODEIMINI GIIZIS:
The Strawberry Moon

PHENOLOGICAL NAMES:
The Rainy Month
The Month of Long Days
The Growing Month
The Month of Summer Solstice

J UNE IS TYPICALLY OUR WETTEST MONTH, but also the month of the most daylight. June often has cool foggy mornings, hot humid afternoons with rain every few days and at least one big storm. In June the wood thrush sings at 4:30 in the morning, and the wood peewee continues until 9:30 in the evening as we celebrate the solstice.

June is a month of growth. Hay making, garden weeding and mowing the lawn every few days. Pollen from pine trees covers the edge of a water-lily bay. Candles of new growth on these same trees give us a pale green against the typical darker green. Lilac, wild rose, raspberry, and blackberry blossoms abound. Roadsides hold daisy, buttercup, hawkweed, and lupine, while the Clintonia, bunchberry, columbine, and starflower fade in the shaded woods. In our gardens peonies and poppies bloom, fresh garden lettuce gives us salads, and rhubarb goes to seed in tall stalks. Strawberries ripening entices us towards the berry season.

June is a month of abundant new life. Baby birds, ducklings, fawns, and bunnies are born. Bobolinks, meadowlarks, and sparrows proclaim their family homes in the fields, while warblers, thrushes, flycatchers, and vireos divide the forest domain.

The painted turtle returns to its origin as it lays eggs on land and the gray tree frog returns to its origin as it lays eggs in water.

Insects show us who really dominates the world. Caterpillars of all shapes and colors eat their way to adulthood. The armyworms strip a forest. Tiger swallowtails, fritillaries, monarchs, and skippers grace our days, while luna and sphinx moths join the fireflies at night. Dew-covered dragonflies and bumble bees work the meadow flowers with spittlebugs and crab spiders staking territory in the flowers. The first cicada calls from nearby trees. In June we have black flies at day, gnats at night, and mosquitoes at anytime.

June exemplifies Nature's energy and enthusiasm bursting into the summer with the excitement of constant news.

June Happenings, The Long-Day Wet Month

What to Look For:

Early June
- full avian chorus in early mornings
- abundance of black flies and mosquitoes
- some years, abundance of tent caterpillars
- birth of fawns
- turtles laying eggs on land
- gray tree frogs calling
- tiger and black swallowtails
- luna moths
- junebugs and ground beetles
- bunchberries, columbine and clintonia in the woods
- lupine and tall buttercups in the open
- pink ladyslipper orchids in the swamps
- false morel
- new tree growth
- pollen from pine trees

Mid June
- most songbirds nesting
- first crescents and fritillaries
- fireflies
- spittlebugs
- orange hawkweeds in bloom in fields
- showy ladyslippers blooming
- iris, water alum, yellow water lilies in wetlands
- blueberry, raspberry and blackberry in bloom

Late June
- avian chorus in early morning and evening
- white admiral and ringlet butterflies
- crab spiders in flowers
- first summer cicadas
- abundance of dragonflies
- daisies in bloom in fields
- white water lilies in bloom in lakes
- ripe wild strawberries
- first sulfur fungus
- early wild roses

THE LARGE MOTHS OF
EARLY SUMMER

J UNE IS A MONTH OF GROWTH. We see it everywhere. Grasses in our lawns seem to lengthen right in front of us. Trees extend their size at this time while ostrich ferns nearly match us for height. New crops of mosquitoes and black flies continue to be active, but they are battled by the new arrivals of dragonflies. Every time we go to a lake or other wetland, we are greeted by more of these rapid fliers.

And the butterflies continue with more kinds. A walk in an open area among the blooming wildflowers reveals new butterflies each day. This insect diversity continues at night as fireflies cause us to take notice of their lights and Junebugs find our lights, bouncing off screen doors. Here too, we might find the largest moths of the northland.

Moths are abundant and diverse. They far outnumber their day-flying cousins, the butterflies. Indeed, moths make up ninety-five percent of the members of Lepidoptera, the order of butterflies and moths. Most fly at night and most are not very colorful. But a few are also out in the daytime. Most are rather small, less that one inch, but four very large kinds emerge in the region now. They are present each year, but more common some years than others.

Interestingly, all are commonly called by their Latin or scientific species names. Luna, polyphemus, cecropia, and promethean. Luna, the best known, is light green while the rest are shades of brown or gray. Largest of our moths, this group may reach a wingspan of six inches. All four are in the same family, often called the giant silkworm moths (though they are not closely related to the famous Asian silkworms). As members of the same family, they share several characteristics. All have large green caterpillars that feed on the leaves of trees.

After much eating in this young stage, they form leafy cocoons placed either on tree branches or on the ground, and here they spend the winter. Emerging in late May or early June, these big adults are rather short-lived. Without mouthparts, they are unable to feed as adults and survive on stored food from their larvae stages.

Adulthood is spent seeking a mate and laying eggs. This is usually done at night. With extended feathery antennae, the males are able to sense the pheromones of the females, and they will frequently fly long distances for such a rendezvous. Unfortunately, lights on our houses, garages, porches, and parking lots may confuse this flight, and many become stranded around out homes flitting around these lights where we find them the next morning, exhausted.

While luna moths are light green, the polyphemus is yellowish-brown, the cecropia is dark with reddish-brown, and the promethean is gray-brown. All have large "eye spots" or some type of deceptive patterns on their wings. This helps to discourage would-be predators. With no ability to eat, their season does not last long. During these nights of late spring and early summer, they seem to be most active. Those of us living in the wooded environments may be visited by these quiet giants. Enjoy such a sight and remember, they cannot bite.

TURTLE EGG LAYING

IN THE WORLD OF NATURE, June is a busy month filled with birth and egg-laying. We usually think of eggs as coming from birds. And rightly so, during this warm wet month, the migrants that stay with us are now beginning their new crop of young. Bird nesting is associated with bird songs, and now is the ideal time to take inventory of local nesters by merely listening to their daily melodies. However, other critters are undergoing egg-laying now too. Among these quiet breeders are the turtles. The northland is home to only two kinds of common turtles, painted and snapping, with a few wood turtles at selected sites too.

Painted turtles are by far the most common ones living here. Most of us know these as the turtles seen sitting on lakeside logs and rocks. Basking at these locations is very important for them. Though they appear to be doing nothing at the time, being in the sun gives them a healthy temperature and needed vitamins.

At this time of June, they travel over land to seek a nesting site. Usually in the afternoons or evenings, the turtles wander up from the wetlands to deposit eggs in soil. (Snapping turtles are more likely egg laying at night or early morning.) Sandy soil is easier to dig in than clay or rocky material, but they have been known to use these sites.

Using only her hind legs and feet, the female excavates a hole a few inches deep. When completed, she drops in the white, oval, one-inch eggs. The usual clutch size is ten, but as many as twenty can be laid with snappers producing more than fifty. Unlike bird eggs, reptile egg shells are flexible and leathery and do not break when dropped.

The mother turtle quickly covers the eggs with soil without ever seeing them. Being in danger on land, she returns to the safety of nearby water. Also unlike bird eggs that need to be incubated by parent body heat, turtle eggs are warmed only by solar heat. It appears that the sex of the baby turtle is determined by temperatures. Warmer eggs tend to develop into females, cooler ones will be males. All hatch in late summer, about seventy to eighty days for painted turtles, maybe one hundred for snappers. Despite emerging from the eggs, the painted ones often do not leave the nest until the next spring. This causes many observers to think that the eggs will not hatch.

Adult turtles are not likely to be eaten by dogs, foxes, skunks, or raccoons, but their eggs might be. Many nests are dug up and devoured. Cars also take their toll, and turtles don't always select the best sites to lay eggs. They have been known to place eggs in lawns, golf courses, gardens, driveways and roadsides. Egg-laying time is, no doubt, a dangerous time for these shelled animals.

If you see a turtle on land during early or mid June, you may be seeing a female seeking a nest and eggs. Leave it alone and watch this terrestrial phase of their aquatic life.

IRISES OF THE WETLANDS

By mid June, the woods is not only shady, it is nearly dark. Only a few flowering plants join the abundance of ferns, mosses, and fungi that can cope with these conditions. The prolific June flora is out in the open at this time. Roadsides and fields are colorful now. The passerby may see quite a show. Daisies give a white backdrop while yellow glows from hawkweeds, buttercups, and sweetclovers. Purple and reds on lupines, vetches, and clovers are scattered among the orange hawkweeds. Many of these plants are not native here and several are not appreciated by all, but when seen now in the summer sunlight, they provide a delightful mix.

But other open sites have flowers too. Out in the wetlands, within the shallows of ponds, swamps, and lakes, plants gather ample sunshine and also give a colorful scene. Floating and flowering at the water's surface, we find yellow pond-lilies (also called bullhead-lily or spadderdock) and white water-lilies. The yellows began blooming in May while the large round-leaved whites have just recently begun to open flowers now that it's June.

Along the shore, white water calla (water arum) has been in boom since May and was recently joined by a display of irises. For most of us, irises are garden plants, and they are blooming there as well. The domestic types have been bred to give a variety of colors, so it's not unusual to see blue, purple, pink, yellow, or white in yards.

Wild irises are a consistent blue, giving them the name of blue flag. The word "iris" means rainbow and we, no doubt, see more of the colors of the rainbow among the garden irises, but a closer look at the wild ones reveals considerable yellow mixed with three large blue petals.

Any one wishing to take that close look will need to wade into water or wet soils to see them. Wild irises stand up to three feet tall. Long wide leaves, almost like those of cattails, reach up beyond the blossoms. Flowers are about three inches across and nearly the same tall. In typical fashion of its family, the flowers are composed of three colorful petals and three sepals. Sepals are only blue, but the petals are blue with yellow in the center. Usually, the plants grow in groups, giving us a dramatic sight of blue as we pass by.

Blue flag iris normally come into bloom during the early days of June. Along with pink moccasin flower, columbines, and false Solomon's-seal, they represent the last of the spring wild flowers. Irises will hold their blue-purple flowers for the next few weeks before fading in the heat of summer. Pollinated plants will develop seeds within a long pod that lasts though much of the fall and winter.

Now, however, they demand out attention as we wander by these wetlands. No other flower here is as blue and as noticeable at the wild iris at this time of June.

Dragonflies (Four-Spotted Skimmers)

THE PACE OF JUNE CONTINUES to quicken as we advance towards the solstice (June 21). With the early sunrise at this time of year, the local songbirds announce their proclamations of home territory while we're still trying to sleep. They find the calm conditions in these early morning hours ideal for vocalizing ownership of their nesting sites. Northlanders interested in bird songs frequently rise very early in June to observe, visually and aurally, these avians.

But June days are full of natural happenings, so that those who choose to sleep late will find much to see as well. The woods is full of late-spring shade-tolerant wildflowers. Blue-bead lily and bunchberry abound in such locations, along with and ever-increasing variety of ferns. Out in the fields, the open-area wildflowers are also beginning their blooming. Hawkweed, daisy, vetch, and yarrow have all begun a notable floral display. In the wetlands, water calla and yellow pond-lily are opening.

And there's more in the sunlight on these clear days of June. This is the time when various insects arrive, and often they warm their bodies by basking in the solar glow. The recently returned monarchs have joined black-and-yellow tiger swallowtails, orange-black checkered fritillaries, whites and sulphurs, even some tiny skippers as butterfly diversity explodes. No early rising needed to watch butterflies. Most don't fly before 9:00 A.M.

Also soaking in the warm sunlight now is the new crop of dragonflies. The dragonfly season began with the arrival of the migrant green darner in April. Its migrating status is unique for these excellent-flying insects. Others stayed in their immature stage under water until late May and early June. Responding to the warmer weather and longer days, they entered adulthood and took wing.

Usually under the cover of darkness, these aquatic larvae select a stick, rock, plant or one of our docks to climb up on. When out of their watery home, their exoskeletons split down the back, and the dragonflies pull themselves from within to begin the winged mature part of their life. Stretching and basking in the morning sunlight, they strengthen their four wings and take flight as though they are used to such mobility.

Species of dragonflies will continue to emerge for the next two months, but some of the early ones bear names as: beaverpond baskettail, Hudsonian whiteface, chalk-fronted corporal, and four-spotted skimmers. It is the last of these that I see often during my June afternoon walks. Sitting quietly on roadside and trailside plants, they spread wings to attain the greatest warmth, but they are also alert to any potential bug meals that come by. From these perches, they dart out, grasping a variety of insects, including mosquitoes. Excellent eyesight and flying skills make these two-inch insects formidable predators.

Instead of looking for four spots on the body, perhaps the best way to recognize the four-spotted skimmer is to see the black tip of the abdomen, the "tail." Soon other species of dragonflies will leave their water immaturity and take to the air, and we'll see many kinds during our summer trips to the lake, but the emergence begins now.

SPITTLEBUGS

WE HAVE REACHED THE SUMMER SOLSTICE (first day of summer) and the time of longest daylight for the whole year. With the sun rising shortly after 5:00 A.M. and setting a few minutes past 9:00 P.M., we experience sixteen hours of its light. Add the conditions of dawn and dusk to this and we have seeable light for nearly eighteen hours each day. Not only is this month the time of greatest daylight, it is also warm and wet. Putting these factors together, June is a month of terrific growth.

Most of us see the results of all this light and growth in our lawns and gardens. Both demand care now if we're going to keep them as we want. Plants make use of this weather and seem to grow right in front of our eyes. But as we watch the changes in our yards, we see that various animals are affected by this season too. A trip around our backyards, roadsides, and parks reveal a plethora of insects. The new crop of dragonflies and butterflies is joined by early cicadas and the first fireflies, and more.

A few days ago as I walked on a woodland trail, I noticed some white frothy material among these maturing plants. Approaching for a close look, I saw that it looked a lot like spit. The time of the spittlebugs has arrived. Each June, we take note of this foam on a variety of plants. Once discovered, I was able to find this phenomenon on about fifteen kinds of plants. The clover family seemed most likely to wear this bubbly attire, but it was also found on goldenrod, tansy, mustard, hawkweed, daisy, and thistle. I expect many other plants as well.

The spittlebug, also known as froghopper because of the appearance of the adult (which most of us rarely see), selects these plants for the young to grow into maturity. It all began with an egg deposited at the plant's base late last summer. Here it wintered.

With the excellent growing conditions prevailing in June, the plants developed new stems, leaves and flowers. And the eggs hatched. The tiny young worked its way up the stem, nestled into a site where the foliage grew and settled down to develop. But it (yes, there is only a single insect here) needed protection. Insect protections are almost as diverse as this group of animals is, but the spittlebug's method is truly unique.

The young (called either a larva or nymph) moves sap through its body, where it mixes with air to create a foamy broth. This covers the body. With such a resemblance to spit, we are likely to leave it alone, exactly what this insect wants. And so, the immature spittlebug is able to feed and grow with limited interference.

Anyone looking inside this wet home will find the minute light-colored young. Left alone in this moist site, the spittlebug will spend the next couple of weeks growing to maturity. And most likely after this time, we will no longer see this foamy material, but we usually don't see the adult either as it finds the right plant to lay its eggs.

CRAB SPIDERS ON FIELD FLOWERS

THE FIELDS, MEADOWS, AND ROADSIDES of late June are a delight to behold. They are filled with the colors of the early summer flowers. Nearly every open space, including some lawns, holds myriads of orange hawkweeds, yellow hawkweeds, tall buttercups, daisies, vetches, lupines, yarrows, sweetclovers, and clovers. Out in the open, the plants find ample sunlight and moisture. Here, too, they can be found by the abundant butterflies, moths, bees and wasps that pollinate these colors of summer.

But as we pass by these flowers, it's worth the time to take a closer look. In nearly every patch of daisies, we can see at least one plant that has been chosen as a hunting site for a crab spider. Crab spiders, a kind of spider that does not make a web, seek out an open daisy as their place to snare a meal. They sit on the flower where the rays meet the central disk. Here they remain motionless with front legs outstretched. In this pose, they resemble crabs; hence their name. To help with the hunting success of this spider as it waits for a meal, the spider is mostly white—blending in with the white of the flower's rays (petals).

In the world of spiders, there are basically three forms of hunting. Many will construct a web that catches unsuspecting insects. Here they wait for their meals to arrive. These spiders are sedentary in their hunting and do little walking. Others do not make webs, but instead use strong legs and keen eyesight to pursue their prey. This is seen with the fleet wolf spiders and the agile jumping spiders. Crab spiders represent a third and less common method of hunting. The spiders remain stationary at one location, relying of food to come to them, but they do not build webs.

As usual among spiders, females are much larger than males. While she is white with colorful pink stripes on her abdomen, he is only about one-fifth her size and mostly dark. Not only does feeding and resting take place on the flowers, so does courtship. It is not unusual at this time in early summer to see both the large white female and the small dark male on the same daisy.

As the summer proceeds and the daisies fade, the spiders will move onto other field flowers in search of insect food. Midsummer black-eyed susans and late summer goldenrods take the place of these early daisies. White rays of daisy are replaced by the yellow rays of black-eyed susans and goldenrods. With a different color background, it would seem that the spider's camouflage hiding place will be revealed. Not so. To compensate for this change, the crab spider is also able to change, varying its color. Thus, it still blends in with the flower's colors. The white spider of June becomes the yellow spider of July.

So what appears to be a colorful bouquet of summer flowers in the fields and meadows of late June is often a location of predator-prey activity as well. And such deceitful hunting will continue throughout the summer.

SHOWY LADYSLIPPERS

PLENTY OF FLOWERS ARE IN BLOOM during the long warm days of June. However, instead of the woodland wildflowers of May, those that add color to these hotter days are mostly in the open. This is the time the fields and roadsides come alive with colors. Yellows of buttercups and hawkweeds mix with the orange hawkweeds and red clovers to make the green fields sparkle with a rainbow. Roadsides also abound with whites daisy and false Solomon-seal. The most obvious plant out in June is probably the lupine. Growing in groups, each one puts up a spike of colored blossoms. Purple is the norm, but blue, pink, and white may be here too. It is hard to keep one's eyes on the road when passing by.

But maybe the most delightful flower in bloom at this time is a bit harder to find. Showy ladyslipper orchids, the state flower of Minnesota, are now adding its pink-and-white charm to swamps, wetlands and damp forests. Growing in such sites and being most common in the northern part of the state, this large orchid, two to three feet tall, is not even seen by many, or most, of the residents of this state.

Those who do trudge into these damp locations and put up with the local mosquitoes will find the experience of seeing showy ladyslippers in bloom well worth the walk. Like their cousins, the pink ladyslippers (moccasin flowers) and the yellow ladyslippers, the showies have a flower of two parts. The bottom is a pouch of fused petals that form a hollow ball-shaped growth. This spherical part is pink. Above this is the white portion that fans out in three more normal looking petals. Stems are long and leafy unlike the basal leaves of the pink ladyslipper orchids and more like the yellow ladyslipper.

In true orchid fashion, the roots grow in a mycorrhizal relationship with soil fungi. This relationship is rather fragile, making them hard to successfully transplant. Added to this is the fact that showy ladyslippers grow very slowly. Plants take nearly twenty years to reach maturity and put forth blossoms. Some years, when it is perhaps too dry, they may not bloom at all.

Our state flower will continue to bloom for a week or two, reaching into July, but it will eventually fade with the heat of summer. Flowers catch the attention of large bees that subsequently pollinate it and, by late next month, seed pods will replace these two-tone blossoms.

Late June, with its heat and annoying insects, may not seem like the best time for a walk. But for those visiting a growth of showy ladyslippers, it is an adventure.

BIRD SONGS OF LATE JUNE

L ate June is the time when we experience heat mixed with a few storms and the latest sunsets of the year. The days following the solstice are very long and the early summer sun is in no hurry to set. This is also the time of plenty of bird melodies.

Migrants arrived nearly a month ago quickly set up their territorial claims and announced them to others through repetitive songs. This is followed by nest building and egg laying. Once the incubated brood is hatched, the young need to be fed very often to satisfy their growing appetites. Nevertheless, adults still find time to proclaim their ownership in song. Many sing hundreds or more times per day, but they still are able to search for and find food within their home sites.

Nearly all of the northland songbirds are diurnal, that is active during the light time of day, usually roosting at night. However, with the activity of an eager participant, many start to sing before sunrise. Any of us rising at that early time, about 5:15 A.M., will find that the songsters have already been up for a while. Some begin singing about one hour to forty-five minutes before sunrise, in anticipation of the sun. These pre-dawn times are just fine for songbirds. At this early hour, winds are calm, temperatures are cool and fewer frogs or insects call, so bird voices carry a longer distance. Most are not enough to wake us though a few woodpeckers use our houses as their site to drum their business and may not be appreciated by those trying to sleep.

Throughout most days in early summer, songs will continue. Many pause at times in the heat of the day but continue later. As the afternoon progresses to evening, the birds return for an encore.

Though most of us are sleeping during the early show, we are awake during the matinee and the late shows. Sunset is now shortly after 9:00 P.M., but seldom does Sol's exit stop the show. Singing slowly lulls until darkness about one-half hour later puts a damper on this activity. It is interesting to note some of the songsters of dawn also perform at dusk.

Early morning songs emanate from sparrows, wrens, robins, vireos, and doves, along with hermit thrushes, wood thrushes, veeries, and a small flycatcher called the wood peewee. Most of these will not sing again in the evening, but the thrushes and wood peewees do.

During the half hour after dusk falls, hermit thrushes and wood thrushes continue their lovely flute-like songs while their cousin, the veery, repeats its rolling phrases. Not to be overlooked, the tiny wood peewee will continue its plaintive "pee-wee" call until the others have finally silenced.

It is not unusual for us to hear this tree-top song until 9:45 P.M. in late June. Frequently, they will still be active as the nocturnal bats take wing. When finally stopped at about 10:00 P.M., the fireflies emerge for a visual show, and we forget the vocal ones.

JUNE
DAILY CLIMATE INFORMATION FOR DULUTH, MINNESOTA

Normal Records

DAY	AVERAGE HIGH	AVERAGE LOW	RECORD HIGH	RECORD LOW	SUNRISE	SUNSET
1	67	45	87/1988	31/1946	5:19	8:54
2	67	45	88/1948*	30/1962	5:18	8:55
3	67	46	90/1948	30/1982	5:18	8:56
4	68	46	90/1968	31/1964*	5:17	8:57
5	68	46	88/1988	32/2000	5:17	8:58
6	68	46	88/1976	33/1897	5:16	8:59
7	68	47	88/1988	34/1934	5:16	8:59
8	69	47	88/2000*	33/1885	5:15	9:00
9	69	47	89/1956	31/1988	5:15	9:01
10	69	48	92/1956	27/1972	5:15	9:02
11	70	48	91/1956*	34/1958	5:14	9:02
12	70	48	91/1956	31/1962	5:14	9:03
13	70	49	87/1987	32/1969	5:14	9:03
14	70	49	90/1910	35/1958	5:14	9:04
15	71	49	88/1913*	35/1989	5:14	9:04
16	71	50	88/1910	35/1982*	5:14	9:05
17	71	50	93/1995	35/2000*	5:14	9:05
18	72	50	94/1995	36/1876	5:14	9:06
19	72	50	95/1933	34/1992	5:14	9:06
20	72	51	88/1995	31/1992	5:14	9:06
21	72	51	90/1911*	30/1992	5:15	9:06
22	73	51	94/1910	37/1972	5:15	9:07
23	73	52	92/1922	35/1972	5:15	9:07
24	73	52	91/1890	36/1979	5:15	9:07
25	73	52	93/1980	39/1957	5:16	9:07
26	74	52	92/1931	36/1982	5:16	9:07
27	74	53	94/1910	37/1925	5:17	9:07
28	74	53	97/1910	40/1968	5:17	9:07
29	74	53	96/1910	40/1992	5:18	9:07
30	75	53	96/1910	36/1988	5:18	9:07

*Denotes latest of multiple years
Average Temperature for June: 60.1 F
Average Precipitation for June: 4.23 inches

JULY

JULY GETS ITS NAME in honor of Julius Caesar. Previously it was called "Quintilis" meaning "five," since it was the fifth month of the year in the old Roman calendar.

AABITA NIIBINO GIIZIS:
The Half Summer Moon

PHENOLOGICAL NAMES:
The Hot Month
The Month of Thuderstorms
The Month of Ripe Berries
The Month of Aphelion

J ULY IS USUALLY OUR HOTTEST MONTH. Mild mornings melt into scorching afternoons that send us looking for shade. We enjoy the fireworks of mid-summer with warm nights, clear stargazing, and a high full moon. July is aphelion when Earth is most distant from the sun in our orbital journey.

July is all about lazy picnics, baseball, and swimming. Lemonade, water melon, and ice cream go down easy. Afternoon thunderstorms remind us of lightning's force and intensity. Hail and tornado warnings keep us aware, with sweat and sunstroke and sunburn also concerns.

Produce explodes in the garden, hollyhocks burst into bloom in the yard, and day lilies count off the season. Half-grown raccoons and fledgling robins draw our attention, the goldfinches continue their late nesting while phebes raise another brood. Little toads hop to adulthood from the pond, while plucking calls of the green frogs persist.

In July the roadside yellows of black-eyed susans and sweet-clovers give way to sunflowers and goldenrods. Yarrow, milkweed, fireweed, and cow parsnip flower in the meadow, with lush ostrich and interrupted ferns grow tall in the nearby woods. July sees the first mushrooms.

July has the early berry harvest. Raspberries, blueberries, juneberries, and pin cherries join strawberries in their bounty, and it becomes a battle between berry pickers and bears to get there first.

A myriad of insects fill the meadows. Grasshoppers and dragonflies join the monarchs, skippers, and fritillaries in the day's heat while early katydids tune up at night. Deer flies and horse flies pick up where black flies left off, and new species of mosquitoes emerge. July is honey-making time with clovers and basswoods buzzing with activity. Cicadas' arboreal trill almost measures the heat. And spider webs are woven at every available site.

But in July, even with so much going on, Nature turns the corner. Shorter days trigger early migrants. Swallows fill telephone wires while restless shorebirds line the beaches. We hear fewer bird songs while the preaching red-eyed vireo tries to convert the season to stay.

July Happenings: The Hot Thunderstorm Month

What to Look For:

Early July
- still plenty of morning bird songs
- fledglings leaving the nests
- green frogs and mink frogs calling
- abundance of tadpoles in ponds
- black-eyed susans, Canada anemones blooming in fields
- twinflower, pyrola in bloom in woods
- pitcher plant blooming in wetlands
- wild rose blooming along roadsides

Mid July
- many fledglings, fewer bird songs
- abundance of butterflies species
- abundance of deer and horse flies
- more cicadas and first katydids
- pennant dragonflies are common
- spider orb webs
- wolf spiders with young on abdomen
- cow parsnip, milkweed blooming in fields
- michigan, wood lilies blooming along roadsides
- jewelweeds blooming in damp sites
- ripe pin cherries
- fern growth thick in woods
- first mushrooms, waxy caps

Late July
- few birds are singing, red-eyed vireo, wood peewee
- tree swallows on utility lines
- early shorebird migrants
- tiny toads emerge from ponds
- fishing spiders on ponds
- wood nymph and northern pearly-eye butterflies
- early goldenrods, fireweeds in bloom along roadsides
- indian pipes blooming in woods
- basswoods blooming
- ripe blueberries, raspberries, thimbleberries, juneberries
- more mushrooms: boletes, russula

THE MONTH OF BUTTERFLIES

THE WARM WEATHER OF LATE JUNE has had quite an impact on the northland. Not only did these conditions bring out an explosive growth among the plants and mushrooms as usually seen a bit later in the season, but it also influenced the insects. The long-awaited mosquitoes made their move, quickly followed by a couple of summer flies, deer flies and horse flies.

But insects in the northland are more that these pesky ones we are so famous (infamous) for. We also now have an abundance and diversity of some better-loved ones: fireflies, dragonflies, damselflies, moths, and butterflies. Sometimes called flying flowers, butterflies may be the most appreciated of all insects.

Here in the northland, July is the month of the greatest numbers of butterflies. Before this hot month is over, we will see butterflies with wing colors of white, yellow, orange, red, blue and some even a drab brown. We will see ones as big as the palm of our hands and others that may be able to sit on our fingernails. Many have mysterious and strange names like sulphur, cabbage, admiral, fritillary, satyr, ringlet, wood nymph, and skippers. But for most of us, it is the large black-and-orange monarch and the black-and-yellow tiger swallowtail we are most likely to know about and look for.

Tiger swallowtails are found throughout the state, but they vary from north to south. The eastern tiger swallowtail is the species of the south, while our northern swallowtail is commonly called the Canadian tiger swallowtail. Both are large and yellow with black stripes (hence the tiger name), but the southern type is a bit bigger.

The name "swallowtail" comes from the long growths on the tip of the hind wings that extend far beyond the rest of the butterfly. This is somewhat like the long tail feathers as seen in the bird, the barn swallow. Besides being named after two kinds of animals, tiger swallowtails are just plain interesting to watch.

Emerging from their winter chrysalis each year in late May or early June, they spend the month with us, often lasting until mid July. As they fly through our yards and parks, they'll visit whatever

137

is in bloom at that time. The list of nectaring plants are cherry blossoms, honeysuckle, lilac, blackberries, raspberries, irises, clovers, and those not in flower until July: milkweed, dogbane, and thistle. Frequently, they fly higher up in nearby trees. Here they place their eggs that will hatch later in the summer. The caterpillars proceed to feed on leaves of aspen, birch, cherry, or willow. It is interesting to note that the young feed at night. By fall, they form a chrysalis in which they spend the winter.

Occasionally, we may find congregations of these large butterflies on the soil, especially at the edge of shrinking puddles after storms. Here they gather moisture and minerals. Often these groups are all males and have been called: "boys at the bar." Seen alone or as many, these beautiful butterflies add much to our summer days.

SPIDER NESTS

ATE JULY IS A WONDERFUL TIME along the roadsides and meadows. Here some of the magnificent flowers of mid summer stand tall and colorful. Purple fireweeds and milkweeds, yellow evening primroses, black-eyed susans, and white cow parsnips and dogbane all get our attention. This is also the time of ripe raspberries and Juneberries in these same sites, and pausing usually means having a snack or two. Among these flowers and berries, is plenty of animal life to see too.

Birds and small mammals try to beat me to the berries. Butterflies of several species take nectar from the abundant aromatic blossoms. They are joined by bees, flies, wasps, and moths. And the predacious dragonflies, also quite varied at this time, scan the scene for insect meals. But as I look, I see leaves folded over at several places. This deserves investigation. When I do, I see another story of summer. Bent and rolled leaves may be the result of caterpillars that build themselves a feeding shelter. Or they are constructed by spiders. In late July, the architects of these bent leaves are often spiders.

As they grow through the warm season, spiders molt. When reaching their final change of attire, they are mature and ready to reproduce. Following mating, females lay eggs, usually in a sac made by their silken threads. (Spiders make several kinds of silk, only some of which are used for webs.) Once placed in such a hold of bent leaves, some spiders will stand by to guard the developing eggs. Sometimes mother is in the hiding place with the eggs.

Recently, I found many of these sites. In a curled milkweed leaf, I discovered a brown crab spider with her eggs. Nearby a similar leaf held a minute jumping spider family. In reed canary grasses, I saw where sac spiders had folded the blades into triangular chambers with eggs and adult inside. But the largest egg cases were those of the nursery-web spiders.

Even their name refers to them building holding sites for the eggs. Adults are not inside. Instead they sit on a nearby stem guarding any would-be predators. These spiders are the largest of the nest builders. With spread legs, they can reach two inches. Brown with stripes allows them to blend in with bark or dead grasses. On the green plants of mid summer, however, nursery-web spiders are easy to see.

The dozen I found were on milkweeds, dogbanes, goldenrods, and raspberries. Females attach threads to the leaves and bend them to create this nursery site for her eggs. Once secure, she sits by (usually below the nest) and watches for danger. As a dedicated mother, she remains here until well after the eggs hatch and the young spiders, known as spiderlings, fill the inside. This does not last long since the young will soon begin to attack each other. To survive their siblings, they must leave home. With plenty of warm days still this season, they will be able to grow before fall. But for now, in mid summer, this is spider mating and nesting time.

BASSWOOD FLOWERS

WE EXPECT TO SEE TREES IN FLOWER in May. Then we can see a half dozen kinds blooming along the roadsides or woods edges. Wild plum, Juneberry, pin cherry, choke cherry, elderberry, and crab apple all contribute white flowers to the greening scene. As we move into June, we add dogwood, highbush cranberry, and mountain maple to the list of flowering trees and shrubs, while the domestic lilacs produce a color and fragrance of their own.

The scene changes when leaves grow out. Quickly the vernal blossoms are a memory. Indeed, many of these same trees are now bearing products of their earlier flowers and pollination. By late July, Juneberries, pin cherries, and elderberries all have had ripe berries and fruits and others are right behind.

We don't expect to see any more flowers in the woody plants, but one hasn't flowered yet, a very large one at that. Unlike others in the woods, basswoods wait until July to open their clusters of yellow-green blossoms. Along with red maple, sugar maple, and red oak, basswoods are one of the largest of deciduous trees in the northland. Most of us recognize this tree by its big heart-shaped leaves, at six to eight inches long, they are probably the largest leaves of any in the forests. Basswoods also have a unique growth pattern whereby they often have many new branches coming off a root and form a multiple of "small trees" surrounding a large one. Such an appearance allows for recognition of the tree even in the winter. With such a thick growth and large leaves, it's easy for us not to see their flowers even when they're in full bloom, as they are in July.

Anyone stopping near a basswood, however, able to see the flowers or not, is likely to hear the sound of buzzing. Bees find the blossoms even if we don't and they scatter throughout the fragrant florets, often towards the tree top. Basswood flowers are a favorite for honey bees. Gathering nectar, they use it to produce much of the sweet-tasting substance they're famous for. Upon hearing these insects, we might look up to notice the clusters of rather small flowers. These groupings contain about five to fifteen tiny yellowish florets. Each is only about one-half inch across with five thin pale yellow petals. The whole cluster opens up towards the ground. Blooms may be small, but they are numerous all over the large tree and provide for much bee food in July. With the warmth of this month, July is when bees are most active.

Once pollinated, the seeds develop through late summer and into autumn and mature as spherical woody growths. These pea-sized seeds hang from a leaf-like bract that serves as a wing when the ripe seeds are dispersed in the wind. They look and fall something like that of a hand glider. Turning brown, the seeds remain all winter.

The year 2009 was remarkable for basswood flowers and seeds. I watched many trees keep a thick seed cover all winter, often making the trees appear to have a coating of cold-weather leaves. This July, the flowers opened early, but many of the trees I've been watching are also loaded with these tiny blossoms, especially those in the sunlight. It looks like this is another good basswood year.

WAXY CAP MUSHROOMS

USHROOM SEASON IN THE NORTHLAND leans toward late summer and autumn. Most of these simple mysterious growths appear during August and September. During wet years these times would be extended in both ways and some years they abound in every forest and lawn setting. But even if the year is not wet, some mushrooms will be seen. And it all begins with a few that appear in the woods and yards during late July.

To most of us, a mushroom looks like an umbrella-shaped plant sticking up out of the ground. What we are seeing when viewing this is merely the fruiting or reproductive part of this organism. However, under the ground lies a large network of threads, known as hyphae. These hyphae may reach for hundreds or more feet and may live here for many years. If conditions are right for reproduction, they will extend these mushroom fruiting bodies above the ground to spread the spores (similar to seeds). If too dry or too cool, the reproducing will be postponed.

Unlike plants, mushrooms usually get nutrition from dead organic matter in the soil (normally, decaying plants). Sunlight is not needed. But moisture is required, so proper wet conditions are needed before we see these structures above ground. Typically, they have a stem that supports a cap with numerous lines beneath it, known as gills. It is between these gills that the spores are formed. When ripe, they drop from the gills, usually falling to the ground.

We tend to think of mushrooms as white or brown, but colors vary widely as do the shapes and sizes. Some, no doubt, are white and brown, but others are yellow, purple, orange, black, green, and red. Some are tiny enough to fit on your fingernails, others may reach the size of a dinner plate.

A brightly-colored small one frequently seen in July, early in the mushroom season, is the red waxy-cap. Often they have both a red cap and stem. If bumped or cut, they will bruise to a darker color. Red with pointed caps is common, but waxy-caps can vary from the red to yellow to orange.

All are small, only a couple of inches tall, and caps may be only one or two inches in diameter. The common name of waxy-caps comes from the waxy texture felt in the flesh by those who crush the small mushrooms. This bright red appearance may be seen now in July, but it is not unusual to see similar growths as we proceed into late summer.

Mostly a resident of the forests where much dead and decaying wood can be found, waxy-caps can be in our lawns too. Here they show the survival of underground hyphae from an earlier time. Late July is when the mushrooms begin. Weather conditions will determine what we'll continue to see in August and September.

EARLY MIGRANTS: TREE SWALLOWS

L ATE JULY IS PLENTY WARM, often the hottest time of the summer, but we still see signs of the season moving on. The sunrise time of 5:45 A.M. is about half an hour later that a month ago. Sunset occurs a bit earlier, with the sun's departure before 9:00 P.M.

Late July is a time of fireweeds, milkweeds, and black-eyed susans in the roadsides, along with the first sunflowers and goldenrods. It is also a time of tall lush ferns in the woods and the first mushrooms in the yards.

We now see more ripe berries — blueberry, juneberry and raspberry — joining the strawberries as mid summer treats, while red baneberries advertise ones that should not be consumed.

Many white-tail bucks now hold velvety antlers overhead while the fawns, often still with spots, follow mommy. Young rabbits, squirrels, and chipmunks are on their own, and the new crop of raccoons joins their parents on regular jaunts.

Among the birds, the young of many species have fledged and now sport a full set of feathers, but still beg meals from the adults. These hot days, frequently referred to as mid summer, do not seem to be the beginning of migration, but the shortening daylight does trigger the start of the southbound trek.

Like many other natural phenomena, migration south starts off slowly but leads to the bigger flights next month. Two unrelated kinds of birds begin the movement now, shorebirds and swallows. Along beaches, we might see small brown sandpipers as they run in the surf. But it is on roadside wires where we are more likely to find this movement as tree swallows line up.

Tree swallows are early birds to return to northland in spring. Quickly they settle into hollow cavities of trees and bird houses to raise their families. By mid July, the young have grown out of the nest and begin to feed with the parents. Eating insects in mid-air, they carry on the fast flights that swallows are well known for.

These feeding families are often seen sitting on utility wires. Soon they are joined by other families. It is not uncommon by late

July that related birds perched here may reach fifty or more. Soon, we may even see about a hundred. They get restless and, one day, we return to these swallow sites and see that they have gone. The migration is happening.

We're still far from the big flights of fall, but as I was reminded recently when I saw a family of tree swallows on a telephone line, the season (and migration), even in July, has begun.

INDIGO BUNTINGS

J ULY IS SUMMER COMING to a greater maturity. All the quick growth of May and June has settled into its fully developed state by this time. Plants take advantage of these days of warmth and long sunlight.

And with the birds, we also notice a change. The migration of spring reached its apex in late May. The local avian residents got into their territorial claims for the breeding season. The long days of June were filled with egg laying, incubating and feeding of nestlings. With meals several times per hour, young birds caused the parents to seek insect morsels constantly. It's a wonder they were still able to sing as often as they did.

But despite the other demands, June was still filled with bird songs. Using their choral strength, they proclaimed ownership to a section of woods, fields, or wetlands. Many times a day, these melodious statements were given.

Any bird observer at this time can detect where birds live and maybe even find the nest by listening for and following the sounds of territorial birds. And so the busy month of June proceeded as the birds filled their days with meals and music.

In July, we see the next step. The nestlings grew rapidly on such a rich insect diet. In July, they continue to grow to the point that they can no longer fit in the nest. The nestlings of June become the fledglings of July. Still needing help from parents to find food, but with developing feathers, they are nearly adult size. Within a couple of short weeks, the new family will be able to fly with the older ones. As a group, they'll move through the area, beyond the former home territory.

With this change in their life, the reasons for songs have passed, the territories break down. In the lives of most songbirds, mid July is when singing ceases. But a few continue vocalizing late in the season. Most notable of these persistent songsters are the red-eyed vireos, yellowthroats, a couple of sparrows, and indigo buntings.

Indigo buntings have been with us since about mid May, but stand out now in July with their continuing songs. Often they're seen while giving the song of paired phrases. Males perch on the top of dead branches, power lines or fences and normally are easy to locate. However, the diagnostic song is less of a recognition factor than its nearly completely blue body. Only about six inches long, this bright color reveals the bird clearly. Singing is done only by the showy male. Females are a drab gray-brown and are often overlooked or misidentified.

Never abundant, but always present, the pleasant little blue birds are a joy to watch and to hear now in July. Even they eventually will stop singing, usually in August. With their family raised, the indigo buntings finally quiet down and move on.

MILKWEEDS

THE ROADSIDE FLORAL DISPLAY of July is quite prolific. Maybe the best example of a July wildflower is the milkweed. Plants stand about three to six feet tall and each plant holds clusters of pink-purple flowers. The name milkweed refers to the white sticky latex-like sap in the stem and leaves. (The easiest way to see this latex is to break off a leaf. Often the liquid will drip rapidly.) The sap may look like milk, but does not taste like milk. Most of us who are brave enough to taste this substance will not go back for seconds. So it is with other critters, since milkweed is usually avoided by mammal herbivores, even though several kinds of insects devour the leaves.

The term "weed" is usually applied to unwanted or out-of-place plants. Many times weeds are plants that have been brought to this country. Though some people may not want milkweeds in their gardens, fields and yards, they are native. Maybe unwanted by some humans, dozens of insects find a haven in these plants. Most familiar of these milkweed-loving insects are the well-known and loved monarch butterflies.

Caterpillars feed on the bitter leaves from the time they hatch until they form a chrysalis. All this early consuming of milkweed leaves makes these striped caterpillars bitter tasting as well and so are avoided by birds. Adult monarchs will take nectar from milkweed plants, but they go to other blooming flowers too. Plenty of other butterflies find these flowers to be aromatic and a source of ample nectar.

Indeed, anyone serious about attracting butterflies to a garden will include milkweeds among the choice plants. While walking among a milkweed patch at this time, I rarely see less than five kinds of butterflies and often as many as ten species. Fritillaries, crescents, admirals, viceroys, and skippers are usually in attendance. The best time for milkweed flowering is also the time when most butterflies are about.

In addition to these flying delights, the plants are also full of ants, beetles, moths, flies, and wasps, along with several kinds of spiders. One red resident is even called the milkweed beetle, a cousin is known as the milkweed bug. Even the tiny avian flyers, the hummingbirds, are frequent visitors to the pink clusters as well.

We are fortunate to have abundant milkweeds in the north-land. Anyone stopping to take a close look at this plant will be amazed by the huge diversity of insects and spiders here during this warm summer month.

JULY RASPBERRIES

URING LATE JULY, we can see many of the products of the season. Among these are in the world of birds. It is not unusual at this time to see a family of birds move through the woods and fields as the young travel with the parents. Also a fairly common sight is the tiny frogs and toads emerging from an aquatic youth and springtime eggs now hopping in local wetlands. In July, they silently move in our yards and gardens as they go about in search of insect meals. But for many of us, late July is seen in the plants as they show their season's products.

Recently while traveling down a country road, I noticed the usual wildflowers expected in July: fireweed, milkweed, evening primrose, thistles, and early goldenrods, but I was quite surprised to see a few asters also in bloom. These plants are normally part of the scene of late summer and rarely flower in July.

I found many berries. Late July is always when we'll see, and often pick, these juicy morsels of summer. Many kinds flourish now. I saw berries of red elderberry, pin cherry, honeysuckle, gooseberry, Juneberry, blueberry, and raspberry. The last three of these I have been harvesting lately since the strawberry season is winding down. Apparently, an earlier start for this crop meant an early end as well. Picking Juneberries, blueberries and raspberries can cause us to take on different poses. Juneberries, also called serviceberries, are small trees, so we need to reach up or bend the branches to harvest the small fruits. I have found many sites where bears solved this problem by breaking down the whole plant. The low blueberries require a bending of ourselves to reach these small delicacies. Raspberries, growing on medium-sized shrubs, make the task of collecting far more of a normal movement for most of us.

Raspberry plants grow from three to five feet tall with rough stems (the source of the "rasp" part of their name) and small spines. These are not like the more powerful thorns of its cousin, the blackberries, but it is best for the picker to be protected. The bright berries are easy to extract from the sepals where they grow on branch tips.

Each soft red fruit contains many small seeds. (Botanically, the arrangement is known as a cluster of drupelets.) The berries are a way of dispersing the tiny seeds. Colored so as to be seen by birds and small mammals, they are found and carried off, usually eaten. Passing through the digestive system unharmed, the deposited seeds will still be able to grow.

It is nice to know that by picking and eating raspberries, I'm doing what nature has designed and that the berry season that we see now in late July will continue for weeks.

JULY
Daily Climate Information for Duluth, Minnesota

Normal Records

Day	Average High	Average Low	Record High	Record Low	Sunrise	Sunset
1	75	54	99/1883	35/1988	5:19	9:07
2	75	54	90/1937	42/1994*	5:19	9:07
3	75	54	93/1990	40/1963	5:20	9:06
4	75	54	95/1881	40/1972	5:21	9:06
5	76	54	94/1886	36/1967	5:21	9:06
6	76	55	95/1988	41/1969	5:22	9:05
7	76	55	100/1936	38/1984*	5:23	9:05
8	76	55	98/1936	37/1961	5:23	9:04
9	76	55	98/1936	42/1997	5:24	9:04
10	76	55	95/1980*	41/1968	5:25	9:03
11	76	55	92/1936	41/1985	5:26	9:03
12	76	55	102/1936	42/1990*	5:27	9:02
13	77	56	106/1936	39/1990	5:28	9:02
14	77	56	98/1901	37/1987	5:29	9:01
15	77	56	96/2006	43/1962*	5:30	9:00
16	77	56	97/1936	44/1958	5:31	8:59
17	77	56	94/1964	40/1971	5:32	8:58
18	77	56	97/1932	43/1984	5:33	8:58
19	77	56	94/1901	43/1971	5:34	8:57
20	77	56	98/1901	42/1966	5:35	8:56
21	77	56	93/1960*	38/1973	5:36	8:55
22	77	56	95/1941	40/1985	5:37	8:54
23	77	56	93/1945	39/1962	5:38	8:53
24	77	56	91/1886	41/2004	5:39	8:52
25	77	56	89/1989*	42/1915	5:40	8:51
26	77	56	92/1930*	40/1991	5:41	8:50
27	77	56	94/1931*	42/1981	5:43	8:48
28	77	56	97/2006	45/1992	5:44	8:47
29	77	56	96/1916	42/1971*	5:45	8:46
30	77	56	94/1995*	42/1992*	5:46	8:45
31	77	56	95/2006	42/1924	5:47	8:43

*Denotes latest of multiple years
Average Temperature for July: 65.8 F
Average Precipitation for July: 3.85 inches

AUGUST

UGUST GETS ITS NAME in honor of Augustus Caesar. Previously it was called "Sextilis" meaning "six," since it was the sixth month of the year in the old Roman calendar.

MIINI GIIZIS:
The Blueberry Moon

PHENOLOGICAL NAMES:
The Month of Foggy Mornings
The Month of Early Produce
The Month of Silent Birds and Singing Insects
The Month of Dog Days

August has cool foggy mornings melting into dog-day afternoons. August is later sunrises, earlier sunsets with the impressive perseid meteors decorating a summer night. August sees the early harvest as we enjoy tomatoes and sweet corn from the garden, raspberries and blackberries from the meadow, and chokecherry jelly from the roadsides. August shows goldenrods, asters, and sunflowers in those same places while arrowheads and joe-pye weeds light up the wetlands.

August sees the songbirds fall silent after their families are raised and preparing for migration. Warbler species gather with local chickadees and vireos as they begin their southbound trek. August has great blackbird flocks in the fields, grouse families in the woods, and loons gathering in lakes. Groups of sandpipers gather on beaches while hundreds of nighthawks circle overhead, and the goldfinches finish nesting.

Insect songs take up where the bird songs left off. Afternoon heat brings out the arboreal trills from cicada with katydids and crickets keeping the chorus going at night as they chirp, buzz, and click in the meadows and fields. Late-season butterflies, bumble bees and wasps feed in the hot days while darner and meadowhawk dragonflies join spiders in dining on insect meals. The first monarchs migrate, moths are attracted to porch lights, and bats hunt at dusk.

Turtles bask, young wood frogs hop from their empty vernal pond home and tree frogs climb on our houses. Huge orb webs hang in the dew-covered mornings and tell of a night of bug catching. Phlox, purple coneflowers, and golden-glow sunflowers replace the daylilies in the yard while new mushrooms show up every day. August sees the first tinge of color in sumac leaves, telling us the season is moving on. Still summer, August's shorter days reluctantly move us toward fall.

August Happenings: The Warm Foggy Month

What to Look For:

Early August
- goldfinches nesting
- warblers beginning to group
- many shorebird migrants
- bird silence, calls from cicadas, crickets, katydids
- clearwing moths
- hornet nests
- bladderworts, arrowheads blooming in wetlands
- evening primrose in bloom
- thistle in seed (down)
- first asters among the goldenrods
- more ripe berries

Mid August
- more migrants
- sphinx moths
- bat mating season
- abundance of goldenrods in bloom
- early asters and sunflowers blooming
- joe-pye weed blooming in the wetlands
- eyelash and coral fungus

Late August
- migrants more common, early raptors
- nighthawks, chimney swifts, warblers
- migrant monarchs
- spring peeper, gray tree frogs calling
- abundance of grasshoppers and locusts
- abundance of spider webs
- goldenrods, asters, sunflowers
- blackberries ripe
- mushrooms being common

LATE-NESTING GOLDFINCHES

B Y THE TIME THAT WE GET TO EARLY AUGUST, we believe the nesting season for songbirds is over. Any nearby nests we observe are empty. The young have matured into fledglings and scattered. A few might have produced a second brood because of damage done to the first attempt or because some, like the phoebe, regularly go for two generations in our northern climate.

Not only is nesting finished by early August, but the south migration has already begun. Tree swallows line up on roadsides wires, and along the beaches and mud flats, shorebirds are getting ready for their move south.

With all this going on, it seems strange that a bird is just beginning its nesting time in early August, but such is the situation of the goldfinch. Two months ago when other songbirds sang and defended home territories, these small yellow-and-black birds flew about with no family chores of their own. Only now have things changed. These carefree finches are settling into raising their brood.

A common bird of the northland, goldfinches are frequently seen in our yards almost anytime of the year. Bright yellow with black wings and tail and some black on the head, they are easy to see. Also known as "wild canaries," the well-loved eastern goldfinch is the state bird of three states. With the coming of winter, they change attire to a more drab coloration, but continue to be with us, a regular guest at our feeding sites.

Birds give a repeated phrase as they fly in their characteristic dipping flight. At rest, they'll sing a long and more complicated song. Like their cousins, the pine siskins, they dine on a variety of seeds. With seed and insect food available now, the goldfinches select a nesting home, usually a small tree or shrub. Here they proceed to build a small compact nest composed of grasses and thistle seed fluff, often called thistle down. Some say that the nest of the goldfinch is so tightly made that it can hold water without leaking.

It is the use of this thistle down that is so important to their nests as to cause them to breed now. Canada thistle is a very common roadside plant with light-purple flowers and spiny leaves. These thistles started to bloom about a month ago and recently they formed their seeds. Made for dispersal in the winds, the thistle down is light and fluffy. It makes good nest lining material and the goldfinches delay their nesting until this proper building material is available.

Now, in early August, after thistle plants have formed their wind-blown downy seeds, these small birds are nesting. With plenty of food and plenty of thistle down, they can expect considerable success, and we can be sure of the presence of goldfinches for the several weeks.

MORNING WEB WATCHING

A CCORDING TO THE CALENDAR, early August is mid summer, but in the north the season is moving on. Later sunrises and earlier sunsets shorten the daylight. We now have nearly an hour less now than we did on the solstice. (By the end of this month, diurnal light will be lessened by another hour and a half!) Days can still be hot, but as we go through August, we'll see much that tells of the impending autumn.

During this summer month we gather much of our garden harvest. Tomatoes and sweet corn become regular parts of our diet, and berry pickers turn their attention to blackberries and chokecherries as the raspberries wind down. We see the first migrating birds and monarch butterflies. The roadsides now are full of goldenrods and sunflowers with a half dozen species of asters scattered about too. Early mornings, with a bit of cooling, carry heavy dew in lawns and fields, mist in wetlands and frequently, a fog covering all. It's these wet mornings that provide a particularly good look at spider webs.

Spiders have been with us since early spring, but several factors make mid to late summer the ideal time to see the abundance of their webs. These eight-legged critters have been growing all summer. Warmer temperatures have been conducive to insect proliferation. More insects mean more spiders. Though many spiders do not make webs, it's those snares we're likely to see in the early morning dew, mist, and fog of August. We never realize how many there are until droplets settle on the threads and allow them to be seen.

Spider webs fall into four categories. The simplest are the cob webs. These look like a haphazard array of threads, frequently seen on our window sills. Sheet webs are constructed to look like a bowl shape, often in shrubs. Out on the lawns are the funnel webs. These are mostly flat to the ground with a hole in the center. The spider sits here. For most of us, though it's the large circular orb webs that we think of as a spider web. (It is interesting to note that even among people who don't appreciate spiders, these dew-covered constructions as considered photogenic and beautiful.)

During my morning walks in August, I find a plethora of all the types of webs. Orb webs and funnel webs may be the most numerous along roadsides and fields, but I am intrigued by the shrub sheet webs as well. (I once found a small spruce that held ten of these webs.) Sheet webs also abound in swamps and marshes and I've often counted dozens in the small leatherleaf plants that grow here. Webs are usually bowl-shaped though sometimes this bowl may be inverted, becoming more of a dome. The tiny spiders that construct them are easily overlooked. The web maker sits under the bowl and waits. Insects getting caught here hit the numerous threads and fall to where the patient predator grabs the struggling prey. While orb webs are often knocked down and rebuilt each day, sheet webs will last for many days or weeks before being abandoned. We are just at the beginning the best web-watching time of the year. For the next month and a half they will be out there in the dew, mist or fog nearly every day.

MUSHROOMS AND CORAL FUNGI

THANKS TO RECENT RAINS, the second half of July was wetter than normal and the long spell of dryness earlier seems to have been forgotten. The effect of this rain has been quite noticeable. Lawns and fields that appeared brown at mid month are now wearing the green apparel that we expect at this time.

As an avid berry picker, I was concerned that the raspberries and Juneberries developing in the arid days would not form into the tasty juicy treats as usual. Rain came just in time, and I have been able to gather loads of berries. I now look forward to a full blackberry crop that will be reaching maturity in August. But the moisture has helped much more than the berries.

Roadside plants are flourishing in August, and I have reveled at the sight of thick growths of fireweed and milkweed in bloom. Early goldenrods add yellow to the scene, and I've even noted the first aster, flattop aster, with a head of white blossoms.

In the woods, the rain has revealed other growths. The strange white plant, Indian pipe, sticks up from the leaf litter and scattered about the shaded sites, mushrooms and other fungi show that their season has begun.

I look for the first of the mushrooms in late July every year, but by August, I see them often. These mysterious growths need wet conditions to thrive. However, during a recent walk in a deciduous forest, I encountered several fungal finds. Right on the trail, I found a red-capped russula. One of our most common summer mushrooms, they grow with a red top over white gills, supported by a white stem. Nearby was a patch of tiny orange waxy caps. The entire mushroom is orange (or yellow). It receives this name by feeling like wax.

Lactarius, mushrooms that exude a white milk-like latex substance, are here too as are the first amanita of the season. Often tall and large with a cap as big as a dinner plate, they usually sport a colorful yellow top with many spots. Mushrooms appear quickly and often fade just as fast, but their time has started, and I'm sure I'll find more.

Not shaped like a mushroom, but in many ways similar, corals now arise from downed trees. I paused while passing a rotting log on the forest floor for a closer look and saw that about ten growths of these small brown corals covered the wood. Named after the oceanic corals due to their shape, I find that they look more like branched bare bushes or shrubs. Spores are produced on the tip of the branches and frequently a minute crown shape can be seen here. Colors are usually brown, tan or yellow, though I have seen purple, and they grow to be about two to four inches tall. Like their mushroom cousins, coral fungi feed on the decaying material so abundant here in the woods and help with the needed decomposition of the forest. Thanks to rains of late summer, they appear to be doing well now in August. And I look forward to more fungal finds.

CLEAR-WING MOTHS

INSECTS ABOUND THROUGHOUT AUGUST. Grasshoppers scatter in the meadows while their cousins, the katydids, scratch out creaking and buzzing tunes. Cicadas whine from the treetops while crickets chirp from the forest floor. At the edge of the lake, large dragonflies patrol their territories, and butterflies claim fields as their own. Deer flies keep us alert in the daytime, while the latest species of mosquitoes take over at sunset.

Among the myriads of these six-legged critters are the moths. Many, such as the armyworm, inchworm, and woolly bear caterpillars are better known in their larval or young stage than they are as adults. Others, like the luna, cecropia, and polyphemus are recognized as adults, but go virtually unknown as caterpillars. One group, the sphinx moths, is familiar to us in both stages.

Large thick green caterpillars, often with a posterior hooked spine, commonly called hornworms, will mature to these fairly large drab-colored moths. The caterpillar's tail end appears to be a stinger, but it's harmless. If this bluffing threat does not protect it from a would-be predator, then it will rear up its imposing head end. This pose some early naturalist with a knowledge of historical Egypt thought looked like a sphinx, thus the common name of these moths.

The larvae feed through the early summer and in August, after pupating, they emerge as adults. With a lot of diversity and variation, the adult moths now are seen. The patterns on the outside of their forewings are often a dull brown or gray, easy to pass by undetected. Underneath are the smaller and more colorful rear wings. These wings are seen as the moths fly and vary from pink to orange to red and add a touch of color to these twilight fliers.

One kind of sphinx moth takes these wing patterns in a different direction. The clear-wing moths have wings outlined with a dark margin, but the inner parts of all four wings are clear. When the moths fly, the wings look totally clear. If that's not enough to set them apart from other sphinx moths, they also fly in the daytime.

In the heat of summer days, they take nectar from flowers like milkweeds. And with a hovering flight, they seem to imitate the feeding behavior of hummingbirds. But this is just one of their imitation tricks. With a furry yellow body, the one-inch moths resemble bumble bees. Many a possible predator has decided against having a bug meal when the critter looks like a bee.

With long tongues, all the sphinx moths reach deeply into the summer flowers for nectar meals. This feeding on the wing continues until the cooler, longer nights halts flower blooming. In August, the moths can be seen both day and night, but the longer nights tell us that cooling times may be on the way.

GOLDENRODS LIGHT UP LATE AUGUST

RECENT RAINS BLENDED WITH SUNLIGHT and consistent temperatures above normal have resulted in luscious plant growths. Whether looking at the garden flowers and produce, or the huge numbers of fungi and ferns in the forests, or raspberries, choke cherries, and hawthorns or the wildflowers of the roadsides and fields, we see that the weather conditions have agreed with the plants in these sites, and they have flourished.

July's milkweeds and fireweeds have faded, replaced by seed forming in August. Their purple colors have been taken up by the roadside asters. These late-season flowers bloom in open sites and being either purple, pink, or white, about ten kinds now show up in the northland. But anyone passing by will also note the dominance of yellows as seen in two groups of flowers, the sunflowers and the goldenrods. Maybe half dozen sunflower kinds are now open here with the robust tall sunflower being the one that stands out above the rest. And there are the goldenrods. To me, this widely diverse group of flowers is really where we see August growing and glowing.

About a dozen species of goldenrods live in the region, though to most of us, they all look the same. Most common of these is the Canada goldenrods. Growing in units (most likely clones), they make up big patches in the roadsides, fields, and meadows. With ample rains and sunlight, they reach four to five feet tall. The long flower heads are filled with bees, wasps, butterflies, and moths. But Canada goldenrod is only one type seen now. Even taller, but not as showy is the giant goldenrod. At the other extreme, gray and hairy goldenrods scarcely reach two feet tall. With thin leaves, the grassleaf goldenrod holds a flattened flower head unlike others. Out in the wetlands is the bog goldenrod. While all these varieties are yellow, we have one white goldenrod also in the north country.

A goldenrod I look forward to finding every August is the zig-zag goldenrod. This unusual name is only one thing that separates this flower from others of its kind. Plants grow about two feet tall and when nearly all of these yellow-flower plants have linear leaves on the stem, those of the zig-zag are more broad, looking something like elm leaves. The unique name refers to a stem that grows in a flexible, bent back and forth manor instead of just straight. But maybe the strangest thing about this late summer flower is where it grows. Not one of the fields or swamps, zig-zag goldenrod is our only member of this group that grows in the woods.

Without getting as much sunlight as those in the open spaces, zig-zag goldenrod is late to bloom. I saw the first Canada goldenrod in bloom this year on July 23, while zig-zag did not open until August 6. Like the others in this family, zig-zag goldenrods will continue to show their bright yellows to the late summer scene for several more weeks. Frosts and shorter days of September will put a damper on this glow, and they will form the fluffy seeds that persist for months to come.

These days are pleasant in late summer and many wildflowers abound, whether asters, sunflowers, or the diverse group of goldenrods, they are worth getting out for a look at their roadside glow.

WARBLER WAVES

B Y THE TIME WE GET TO THE END OF AUGUST, the fall migration of birds is well underway. Not only are shorebirds passing by on beaches and nighthawk flocks moving overhead, but also early raptors are already going by Hawk Ridge. Often we see such movements as groups of birds near us. Examples of these gatherings abound: robin families crowd our yards, blackbirds form large flocks in fields, loons out on lakes, and the diverse and active warbler waves.

Several species of warblers have been with us throughout the summer. They arrived back during May and then proceeded to nest and raise their families. These breeding warblers traveled north with others that did not nest here, but kept going further north to the boreal forests. Each year, we host twenty-six kinds that show up here in spring either to breed or to migrate through. Many ardent birders try to find all these kinds each year. Singing often and in full plumage, these little birds put on quite a show in spring. For a couple of weeks, they seemed to be everywhere.

Now the fall flight is upon us. Unlike the earlier one that went north, this southbound trek is made up of silent adults and young, many of which are in a garb differing from spring. With these conditions, the fall warblers are harder to see, making it more difficult to note their passing.

Fortunately, flocks form by families of one species gathering with those of another. Perhaps they find safety in numbers or it is just easier to locate food with a group. These warblers are frequently joined by migrant red-eyed vireos and local chickadees and nuthatches. Though not in song, the birds regularly give communicating calls as they feed and fly. By listening for these calls from the chickadees, nuthatches, and warblers, one can locate the flocks and search the trees for glimpses of the different kinds.

Warblers are usually on the move. To see them, the watcher needs patience, persistence and a good pair of binoculars. But it is not uncommon to find ten kinds sharing a feeding site at this time.

Warblers like the locally breeding black-and-white, chestnut-sided, black-throated green, Nashville, and redstarts will be joined by blackpoll, Blackburnian, Tennessee, orange-crowned, and Canada warblers. Only some of the adult birds are in the attire of early summer, but enough are to allow us to recognize them. And once again, the challenge is to see all twenty-six kinds as they move to the south.

The movement of these flocks, often called warbler waves, continue for several weeks in August into September, pausing at the end of the month. The bird migration we experience here in the northland is worthy of note and observation since very few other places in the country sees this much diversity of warblers twice a year.

BATS OF LATE SUMMER

T HESE SUMMER NIGHTS are warm and calm. They are alive with all sorts of critters. The usual nocturnal rabbits, porcupines, foxes, and deer move about and feed now. Owls call and search for meals. Good numbers of insects, like moths and beetles, silently go about their business, while crickets and katydids add sounds of courtship and territory claims to the darkness. Meanwhile, the opportunistic spiders gather plenty of midnight snacks. Others out feeding at this time do so on the wing.

Bats, the only flying mammals, come out each night at dusk and spend several hours gathering a bellyful of bugs. Seven species have been recorded in the northland. They range from the large silver-haired bat to the tiny eastern pipistrel (also known as the tri-colored bat). Others include the red bat, hoary bat, northern bat, big brown bat, and little brown bat. Some roost in trees and rarely make use of human dwellings, while others are often in our buildings. A few are social, living in colonies, others are loners. But all have one thing in common, they feed on large numbers of insects each night. On some evenings and nights, this may translate into dozens of mosquitoes per bat. Such feeding frenzies usually happen during the dark hours and without us seeing their predation. Insects selected besides mosquitoes include moths, midges, and other night-flying bugs out on these warm summer nights.

Food is found with the use of a system called echolocation. Sounds sent out from the bat bounce off the flying insect and come back to the bat, telling the location of the food. The flying predator is able to find and dine. Huge ears allow this system to work. Eyes are small, but bats can and do see.

Most of us usually encounter two kinds of bats: big brown bats and little brown bats. Both regularly roost in buildings during the day and leave at dusk to feed, often over lakes, ponds, and rivers. After nocturnal meals, they return to their shelter by dawn.

These flying bug zappers have been active since spring, but now, in August, bats become more energetic. In late summer, bats go through mating rituals. Their nightly flights take them to caves, mines, or buildings where they gather in large flocks for mating before the chill of autumn sends them on scattered migrations.Though mating occurs in late summer, fertilization does not happen until the next spring. Females are able to store viable sperm throughout the winter. After a gestation of fifty to sixty days, they give birth in June.

Most of the northland bats will soon be migrating or going into a winter shelter. Through the cold times they enter a torpid state similar, but not identical, to hibernation. Some winter movement does happen, but not enough to use up the valuable stored food that allows them to survive until spring.

With a limited number of bat species in the northland, it may be a bit of a surprise for us to know that bats are widespread and very common throughout the world. About twenty percent of all kinds of mammals are bats, a little more than one thousand species.

With earlier sunsets, these August nights may be the best time of year to see our bats.

CHANTHERELLES

IT'S MID AUGUST. THIS MEANS shortening days, cool early mornings, warm afternoons and, this year, plenty of moisture. Putting these weather conditions together, we have a situation that is ripe for the proliferation of mushrooms and many are here now.

Those of us who make note of these fascinating fungi every year have realized that though they are a phenomena of late summer, their numbers are highly dependant on the proper amount of rainfall. I found several large growths of the orange-yellow sulphur fungus (chicken of the woods) already in June. The backyard and nearby woods was crowded with a variety of mushrooms in July and with the continuous moisture, they are thriving in the woods of August.

For the last couple of weeks, I have not been able to walk in the woods for more that a couple of minutes without seeing them. Mushrooms, a kind of fungi, are a strange form of life but very widespread and diverse. Still they have some things in common. Fungi are not plants. They do not have leaves and can survive well without sunlight. With many thin fibers in their bodies called mycelia (this is why the study of fungi is called mycology), they quickly absorb water and pop up from the ground rapidly. We even have a verb, "mushrooming," that means quick growth. Most of the mycelia stay underground all year, but when the time is right, usually in late summer, they send up a reproductive structure we call a "mushroom." This growth is only used for reproduction, forming spores under the cap, and can be cut, stepped on or eaten without hurting the whole organism, most of which remains below the surface.

At this time, we don't even need to leave our yards to find mushrooms. They come to us. One of the most common seen now is the Russula. (Though mushrooms frequently have common names, they are so diverse that, usually, the Latin name is used.) A red cap with a white stem, often in groups, define them. Nearby we might see Hygrophorus (waxy caps) that show an entire body color of red, orange, or yellow. Amanitas vary from yellow to brown to white, many with large caps. Sometime, in good conditions, they may hold a cap the size of a dinner plate! Another white one, Agaricus (meadow mushroom) does well in open spaces too of late summer. They are very similar to the mushrooms of pizza and salads.

Those who choose to dine on these fungal foods and go out to collect them have a vast knowledge of what to pick and not pick. Many are edible and choice, but others are not and some maybe even dangerous. A sought-after one that makes any mushroom consumer take note is the chantherelle. Yellow-gold and frequently growing in large numbers on the forest floor, they are a delight to behold. Like a few other discoveries, such as a good blueberry patch, chantherelle sites are usually not given away. Conditions have proved well this year and in early August during a single walk, I found five such locations! I assume they are now thriving in many other places among the deciduous tree as well. Whether we add them to our meals or just want to look at these fascinating fungi, the chanthelles light up the woods now and add much to the diversity of late summer's forest fungal flora.

AUGUST
DAILY CLIMATE INFORMATION FOR DULUTH, MINNESOTA

Normal Records

Day	Average High	Average Low	Record High	Record Low	Sunrise	Sunset
1	76	56	97/1930	41/1905	5:49	8:42
2	76	56	93/1930	42/1973*	5:50	8:41
3	76	56	91/1893	39/1971	5:51	8:39
4	76	56	92/1989*	38/1972	5:52	8:38
5	76	56	93/2001	40/1992	5:54	8:37
6	76	56	94/1930	40/1975	5:55	8:35
7	76	56	95/1949	38/1972	5:56	8:33
8	76	56	94/1887	42/1964*	5:57	8:31
9	76	55	92/1958	42/1972	5:59	8:30
10	76	55	90/1947	41/1967	6:00	8:28
11	75	55	94/1947	37/1982	6:01	8:27
12	75	55	89/1965	42/1990	6:02	8:26
13	75	55	91/1970	37/1964	6:04	8:24
14	75	55	93/1961	36/1964	6:05	8:22
15	75	55	92/1930	35/1976	6:07	8:21
16	75	55	91/1988	35/1976	6:08	8:20
17	74	55	91/1934	39/1981	6:09	8:18
18	74	55	92/1955*	38/1975*	6:10	8:16
19	74	54	94/1976	37/2004	6:11	8:14
20	74	54	89/1976	36/2004	6:13	8:12
21	74	54	90/1976	37/2004	6:14	8:11
22	73	54	87/1969	39/1967	6:15	8:09
23	73	54	94/1947	36/1977	6:16	8:07
24	73	53	94/1948	35/1977	6:18	8:05
25	73	53	95/1888	40/1950	6:19	8:03
26	73	53	93/1937	36/1968	6:21	8:02
27	72	53	92/1984	32/1986	6:22	8:00
28	72	53	91/1984	34/1982	6:23	7:58
29	72	52	91/1961*	33/1976	6:24	7:56
30	71	52	95/1961	38/2009	6:26	7:54
31	71	52	92/1961	33/1970	6:27	7:52

*Denotes latest of multiple years
Average Temperature for August: 64.3 F
Average Precipitation for August: 3.70 inches

SEPTEMBER

SEPTEMBER GETS ITS NAME from the Latin word "septem" meaning "seven." September was the seventh month in the old Roman calendar that had ten months. With the addition of January and February, it became the ninth month.

MANOOMINKE GIIZIS:
The Wild Rice Moon

PHENOLOGICAL NAMES:
The Cooling Month
The Month of Red Leaves
The Month of Hawk Migration
The Month of Ripe Fruits
The Month of Autumnal Equinox

SEPTEMBER HAS SHORTER DAYS and cooling temperatures that usher us into the autumnal equinox. Warm and hot summer-like days in the beginning become frosts and flurries at the end. September means back to school, with football and soccer replacing softball and swimming. September is repleat with cucumbers, melons, and apples. Leaf color changes. Reds from dogwood, red maples, sumac, and Virginia creeper blend with yellows of birch, basswood, and sugar maple, setting a backdrop for watching the migration. In September low-flying sharp-shinned hawks and merlins migrate, as the flocks of broad-winged hawks "kettle" (circle on updrafts) at incredible heights and numbers. September sees fall warblers, flickers, and sparrows also moving on, while monarchs and darners remind us that insects migrate too.

Hundreds of orb webs can be seen in the dew-covered and foggy fields, while grasshoppers, katydids, bees, and wasps abound in these same fields later in the day. Slugs, toads, and sphinx moths frequent the garden, with hornet nests on our garage. Ants perform their only flight of the year in the yard.

Waterfowl feed in lakes by day, herons, raccoons, and muskrats by night. Whirligig beetle populate those same waters and the giant water bug disperses from here in a nocturnal flight. Coyotes call.

Asters and goldenrods linger, but fade with the lessening sunlight. Their fluffy seeds change the meadow scene. September is mushroom time. Each day we see the new growth of these remarkable organisms as they decorate the woods and our unmowed lawns.

September shows summer changing it attire as it welcomes the fall with a whole new cast of characters.

SEPTEMBER HAPPENINGS: THE COOLING MONTH

What to Look For:

EARLY SEPTEMBER
- migrant songbirds
- migrant flickers
- migrant green darner dragonflies
- migrant monarchs
- winged ants dispersing
- pelecinid wasps
- yellow jackets
- bee flies on goldenrods
- abundance of funnel webs in fields and roadsides
- abundance of goldenrod, asters, sunflowers
- ripe choke cherries and highbush cranberries
- milk and red-cap mushrooms

MID SEPTEMBER
- peak of broad• winged hawk migration
- sandpiper migrants
- crickets calling
- running crab and jumping spiders
- abundance of orb webs in fields
- beginning of tree leave colors
- inky cap and fairy ring mushrooms

LATE SEPTEMBER
- migrant sharp-shinned hawks and turkey vultures
- garter snakes moving to wintering sites
- giant water bugs dispersing at dusk
- peak populations of water striders and whirligig beetles
- sheet webs in swamps
- gentians in bloom
- peak tree colors, phase I; reds: red maples, sumac, Virginia creeper; yellows: birch, sugar maple, basswood
- ripe acorns and hazel nuts
- honey mushrooms

NIGHTHAWKS

D AYLIGHT CONTINUES TO DIMINISH each day now that we've entered September. With the sun rising at about 6:30 A.M. and setting at 7:45 P.M., we are getting only about thirteen hours of light. We are quickly moving towards the autumnal equinox, the season of fall. We see and feel the effects of these shorter days all around us now. Early mornings hold a lower temperature than the summer, and we grab a jacket before we step outside. The garden plants are reaching maturity, along with the apples. And other trees now hold touches of color associated with this new season.

Taking a closer look at how nature is coping with the shorter cooler days, we see that the fall migration has begun. Traveling all the way to the Gulf of Mexico and beyond, many of these flying critters need to start in August with massive movement throughout September. Sparrow flocks are coming through, but these brown birds, often on the ground, avoid detection. Flickers, brown woodpeckers of the northland, move through the region at this time too. Others are more obvious.

It is hard to not see the large and loud skeins of Canada geese on their flights. Hawks circle over, and from Hawk Ridge we're able to view many. Recently, I watched flocks of shorebirds scamper along the beach of Park Point. But I was able to witness a large flight a few days ago that was a true marvel of migration. While walking during the waning light of evening, I looked up to see the diving, twisting, turning flight of many mid-sized birds. Looking a little closer, I could see the dark bodies and pointed wings each of which held a white mark. This was a flock of nighthawks on their way to winter in South America.

A good example of a confusing name, nighthawks are not hawks. They lack the hooked beak and talons of raptors. Instead, the birds possess a small wide mouth, making for insect catching in mid air. And their flight patterns illustrate how capable they are at such feeding. Not being a species of hawk, they're in a group of birds called nightjars, close cousins to the well-known whip-poor-wills.

The flock that I saw contained about thirty individuals, a good number, but much less than the hundreds seen in past years. Populations of this bird appear to have diminished greatly. However, others reported seeing bigger flocks. At Hawk Ridge, they were noted and counted each day, often in the hundreds.

It was great news to see these nighthawk flights and to hear of others seeing large numbers of them too. Perhaps we will once again see them feeding at dusk and hear their "peent" calls as they circle overhead. And maybe flights like those I saw last week will be the norm each year as we reach this time of late summer.

The Darting Darners of September

EARLY SEPTEMBER IS A TIME of many northland events. Berries, fruits, and produce ripen. Mushrooms abound in the woods and, here too, we see early fall leaf colors of reds and yellows in a few trees. Among local wildlife, it's often a time of migration.

Probably the site most famous and user friendly for viewing this annual movement is Hawk Ridge. Wide panoramic views give the observer a great opportunity to watch avian flights. Best known for seeing raptors, the ridge is also a terrific place to see a plethora of other birds taking their annual fall trips. A few hours spent here looking out on a September day can reveal a continuous succession of sharp-shinned hawks, huge kettles of broad-winged hawks and a mixture of several other hawks, ospreys, vultures, and eagles. Other birds put on a show as well. Flocks of blue jays, crows, waxwings, and geese pass over, with a diversity of sparrows, finches, and warblers coming through often enough to keep us constantly looking. But not all the migration at this time is done by birds.

These mild days bring flights of two kinds of insects heading to the south as well—monarch butterflies and green darner dragonflies. Though often seen, sometimes numerously, at Hawk Ridge, we don't need to go there to find them. Not a day goes by in the last two weeks that I have not seen these critters passing by. The orange butterflies usually flutter by alone, though they often congregate in large numbers while roosting. The green darners, one of our largest dragonflies, is much more gregarious and normally migrate in flocks. I have seen groupings that appear to number in the hundreds. Such was the situation when I went for a bike ride recently on a nearby trail on a clear warm day of late August. The large insects were never out of sight, and they performed their darting, hovering, maneuvering flight constantly. Obviously, they were feeding as they proceeded south. I see their large numbers now, late in the season, as a sign of successful breeding during the warm, wet summer months.

Not all green darners look the same. Some show a sexual dimorphism: females are green, while males have a blue abdomen. Most of the flights now are composed of juveniles and looking much like the females.

Other dragonflies remain on the landscape, and I noted Canada and lake darners as well, as small meadowhawks (males are red, females yellowish-green).

Wintering flights of monarchs are well known and researched. Those leaving us now are headed for a Mexican mountain refuge where their great-grandparents spent the cold season last year. Green darners' cycle is a little less understood. They fly to states further south and there go through another breeding season. When spring arrives, the young head north again. Consistently, they are the first dragonfly of the season every year. Regularly, I see their appearance about April 20.

Like the other migrations concurrently taking place, the green darner flight is on the move. By late in the month, they will be hard to find. But for now, let's enjoy these mild days of September and the diverse flights, bird and insect that come by.

THE WHIRLIGIG BEETLES OF SEPTEMBER

W E HAVE BEGUN THE NEW SEASON OF FALL. The equinox was the night of the twenty-second and twenty-third of September this year (the same as the full moon). Now the hours of darkness are more than those of light, as it will be for the next six months.

Preparation for the impending chilly temperatures abounds in the northland, and we see this happening each day. Trees have put on their autumn attire as they await the massive leaf drop of October. Ripening apples join other fruits and berries maturing now. Lingering summer wildflowers are fading, but new batches of late mushrooms adorn the woods. Overhead, we see plenty of migrants. The hawks and other raptors continue their southbound trek. Every morning and evening Canada geese tell us of their journey as well. And in our yard, we observe groups of blue jays, sparrows, thrushes, and a few warblers.

This is when I like to visit the bay of a nearby lake and watch the season changes there. Lake water is still relatively warm, with freeze-up nearly two months away, but changes are starting here in this aquatic world too. I have been watching a pair of young loons that grew up on the lake this summer. Now, with the adults gone, the youth rest, feed and grow for their flight they'll be taking soon as the water cools. A few ducks come by to rest. The local kingfishers, sandpipers, and herons are finishing their rounds before going. And then there's the insects. Through much of September, the surface of this bay is alive with the movement of small insects called whirligig beetles. Their strange name is appropriate. When threatened or scared, they go through gyrating motions, making them hard to see or capture. They can dive under water or take flight, but they usually do neither, being more willing to stay on their surface sites. Only about one-half-inch long, dark in color and shaped like an oval, they are well adapted to this wet world. A plethora of insects swim in this scene but nearly all are subsurface. And while aquatic insects usually have developed back legs for swimming,

185

whirligig beetles use powerful front appendages to make their circling motions. Here in the protection of the bay, they spend the summer days feeding. They are predators of any small invertebrates available. Staying in one location for much of the day, they go out at night on long travels around the lake. I've noticed many days when the bay is full of their kind, but they're absent the next day. With such small bodies, their treks are, no doubt, quite a challenge, but with the calming of winds, as usually happen in evening, they move as far as they can. With the coming daylight, they find safe harbor in bays, coves or even behind downed logs to wait out the winds, often in other parts of the lake.

Much of the summer is spent with the addition of the new crop for this year. The young hatch in spring. After the immature stages, they emerge in summer. Molting frequently, they reach the size of the adults by late summer. By September, the population of these gyrating insects in the bay is at its peak. Now they prepare for the autumn changes in their own way. Moving about the waters, they gravitate in the shallows and near shore where these water-borne insects — never having lived any time on land — spend winter in a dormant stage in mud and aquatic plants. Like the woods, the bay shows more seasonal preparations as we get cooler.

HAWTHORNS

A NYONE TRAVELING IN THE NORTHLAND in September will find
it hard not to notice the changing tree-leaf color. Along with
the migration and apple ripening, this changing arboreal
attire is a result of the shorter cooler days. Maples have joined the
scarlet glow begun earlier by sumac, dogwoods, and cherries. As
we proceed through the rest of the month, the show broadens and
yellow-gold will help to light up the scene. Indeed, this fall foliage
is one of nature's major events that we enjoy seeing each year.

Red seems to be the color of choice and as I wander along
the woods edge now, I see ripe berries and fruits of sumac, highbush
cranberry, crab apple, and mountain-ash. All hold brightly colored
fruits as a way of getting the attention of passing animals. Red
stands out now in these trees and by being noticed, it is more likely
that the fruits will be picked and consumed and, therefore, spread
the seeds, a form of animal dispersal. Birds, squirrels, raccoons,
bears, and deer all do their part to move the ripened seeds to new
locations.

Red among the green leaves is easy to see, but I find the
hawthorns often carry this a step further. These small trees produce
little apple-like fruits (some people call hawthorn "haw apples") on
branches that also hold long sharp thorns: hence the name. But
hawthorns advertise their product more than other trees. Not only
are these small "apples" bright red, but the trees also shed their
leaves very early. On a tree bare of leaves, the diminutive reds are
quite easy to find. Though nearly all the deciduous trees drop leaves
as we move into October, the hawthorns lead the way with a foliage
drop already in early September. (The hawthorn group is wide and
diverse. Not all kinds have such a quick defoliation.)

Back in late May, the hawthorns helped to color the roadsides and forests margins with clusters of white flowers on the
thorny stems. Along with wild plum, cherries, juneberry, and elderberry, they show just how common such small trees are in the region
when they flower. The plants, like many of the others mentioned,

are in the rose-apple family and the white blossoms provide a fragrance that brings in a plethora of pollinators. Through the summer the fruits are formed. Now trees are loaded with these half-inch products. Beneath the red skin, each hawthorn fruit holds large seeds.

The colorful attention-getting scene works well, and I find hawthorn trees so full of fruits in September that it's hard to imagine they will be virtually devoid of them in a couple of months. Few humans eat these "haw apples." For us they just add more color to the trees of late September.

RED LEAVES OF SEPTEMBER: VIRGINIA CREEPER

DESPITE THE WARM TEMPERATURES and abundant sunlight, the days continue to get shorter. This week we experienced the autumnal equinox and, with it, we stepped into the new season.

One of the most dramatic events of fall is the color change in the trees. Standing green among us for months, many now wear leaf coats of yellows and reds as they prepare to drop their leaves for the winter. Warm temperatures can delay this arboreal performance, but we are still likely to observe plenty of colors on our woody neighbors.

We will see a variety of hues, but basically they are yellows and reds. The scarlet scene may grasp us stronger, but it is the yellows and golds that outnumber these bright ones. Yellow shows up in the leaves each fall as the shorter amount of daylight triggers the trees to break up the chlorophyll, the green substance in the leaves. With the warm season winding down, trees will soon be shutting off production of foods, and so the chlorophyll will no longer be needed. In the absence of the green pigments, leaves turn yellow. Xanthophyll, the yellow pigment, was present in the leaves all summer, but it was masked by the dominant chlorophyll green. When the green goes, the yellow shows up. And it abounds now in ash, basswood, birch, elm, mountain maple, and poplar with sugar maple and aspen soon to join in.

The red pigment, anthocynin, needs to be produced by the leaves at this time. Made from excess sugars in leaves, therefore, it is seen in fewer trees. Red maple, dogwood, sumac, pin cherry, and hazel stand out at this time. Another very common plant with red leaves is not a tree, but a vine called Virginia creeper.

Also known as woodbine, Virginia creeper is a clinging climber. It September, when its leaves turn red it can be seen all over the northland. On a recent drive through several miles of the neighborhood, I saw the bright red leaves of Virginia creeper holding onto walls of buildings, fences, and high among the leaves and branches of trees. Nearly all were glowing and easy to behold. Even those on the ground were wearing some red. These vines were with us all summer but being green like most other plants they did not grab out attention. Bright colors changed all that. Leaves are about six inches long and hold five partially toothed leaflets. (With five leaflets, it is not likely to be confused with the three of poison ivy, that are also red now and also a vine.) And among the noticeable leaves are the purple berries, also of the season. Like other plants of a scarlet glow, the best colors are in sunlit sites. Apparently plenty of light is needed for the plant to make the reddish pigments. A red maple may be crimson in the sun, but yellow in the shade of the woods. The same is true for Virginia creeper.

Take advantage of these next couple of weeks and get out to see the dazzling display as trees and vines wear yellows and reds, with orange and purple thrown in. Autumn is giving us a finale worth waiting for.

THE ORTHOPTERA OF LATE SUMMER

A DRIVE ALONG ANY NEARBY ROAD reveals the changing season. Though some years are wetter than others, a great deal of arid grasses and often plenty of dust is common in September. The mushroom population that flourishes in wetter years can be more limited in dry ones. Searchers need to look harder to find them then. Regional lakes, ponds and swamps are often low, affecting all their flora and fauna.

While dryness may not be premium conditions for much of the northland, some critters always manage to do well. Late summer is the time of insect maturity. The deer fly, horse fly, butterfly, and dragonfly times are mostly past, but their places are taken by the Orthoptera. This word meaning "straight wings" is applied to crickets, katydids, and grasshoppers that now abound in our fields and meadows. Getting enough needed moisture from plant foods, these herbivore insects are easy to see and hear at this time.

During the warm days, meadow katydids and ground crickets call out their mating tunes. With the coming darkness, they are joined by the larger bush katydids and field crickets (some of which may also come into our houses). Both the dark crickets and the green katydids are much easier to hear than to see.

The third members of this group, the grasshoppers, are easy to see. Though they do scratch out sounds, they are much quieter that the katydids and crickets. Anyone walking through tall grasses or along roads or trails near fields will see plenty. Some are green, others gray or brown or combinations. Some hop, others fly. Grasshoppers with us now survived last winter as eggs in the soil. With the warming temperatures, they hatched. These tiny versions of the adults went through several molts as they matured through the summer. Now we see adults with fully developed wings.

Late in the season, they breed and lay eggs after dispersing earlier in summer. Females possess long abdomens to force eggs into their subterranean nest. Eggs are often less than one inch below the surface, but here they are still able to survive most of the cold.

Basically two kinds can be seen here, true grasshoppers, those that hop and do not fly and the locusts, which are more likely to fly when disturbed. With dark wings bordered by light yellow, some locusts have been mistaken for mourning cloak butterflies when flying. It is easy to see the difference when they land and they often produce a clicking sound in flight, unlike the silent butterflies.

Whether jumping or soaring, these insects will be with us as the autumn progresses. Some will linger into October. Eventually stopped by the frost, they are now an interesting addition to September.

THE FALL RAPTOR MIGRATION

ROBINS, FLICKERS, AND BLUE JAYS move through the trees of our yards each day now. In the nearby woods and fields, we can observe several kinds of warblers and sparrows as well. In addition to all this movement, the wetlands hold various water birds, the most obvious being the large, loud Canada geese with flocks of blackbirds and grackles along the edges.

All these birds are moving in their annual southbound trek that we call migration. If all goes well, they will winter in the southern states or proceed to Mexico and Central America. Many will be returning next spring.

Though migrants are passing by now, it is the raptors (hawks, eagles — often referred to as birds of prey) that get most attention in September. Each year at this time, Duluth plays host to birds and birders from other states who come to view the publicized flight at Hawk Ridge. Few leave disappointed.

Occasionally days see many thousands dotting the skies over the ridge. By far most of the hawks on such days are the medium-sized buteos, broad-winged hawks. Huge circling flocks called kettles ride the rising thermals along the shore of Lake Superior, giving altitude to their migration.

Also abundant, but not in such large flocks are the small sharp-shinned hawks, American kestrels, and the larger red-tailed hawks and bald eagles. Not sought out quite as much, but also a regular flier over Hawk Ridge (and many other northland sites) is the turkey vulture. The only vulture in the northern part of the country, some turkey vultures even nest in the region's hills and bluffs.

The birds are nearly all black and with a wing span of about five and half feet, they are one of the largest migrants seen here in the fall. Like others of their kinds, turkey vultures are scavengers and get the bulk of their needs from carrion.

Our usual sighting of this bird is along the roadsides where they feed on dead wildlife, usually mammals that were victims of the traffic. With no feathers on their heads, they are well adapted to feeding on these decaying critters. Head feathers would just get in the way. Without feathers, the head appears as red, thus the turkey part of the name.

Turkey vultures soar with ease through the skies and appear to flap wings infrequently. Occasionally, they ride thermals as the broad-winged hawks do. With a small head, pulled back, a dark body and wings held in a V-pattern, the turkey vultures are easier than most of the raptors to identify as they glide over in their trip south.

Turkey vulture migration peaks in late September, but wanes through the coming weeks. Don't be surprised if during the next couple of weeks one can see these large birds, maybe in sizeable flocks, as they move to the south.

MILK MUSHROOMS

L ATE SEPTEMBER IS MARKED by a beautiful display of leaf color. Mild days and chilly nights in less daylight brings on active movements of bird migrants. Also a regular part of September happenings are the appearance of mushrooms. Rains followed by mild days bring a proliferation of these strange growths to our yards and woods. Absorbing available moisture, they rise up rapidly, and we often see fully developed mushrooms among the lawn grasses where there was none just a couple of days ago. And they appear in huge diversity.

On a recent walk through the colorful woods laden with red and yellow leaves, I noticed much to see on the forest floor as well. Here I saw about a dozen kinds of mushrooms. These ranged from having a cap about the size of a fingernail to those nearly as large as a dinner plate. Caps of mushrooms are usually the colorful part and they showed various colors: white, gray, brown, yellow, orange, red, and even purple. Mixed with these typical umbrella-shaped mushrooms were fungi of other types: red cups, blue-green stain, corals, fingers, slime mold, puffballs, and solid shelves on tree trunks. Though all were getting nutrition from rotted wood, most were not growing on dead logs, though a few did. Many grew as individuals while others were in large clusters of twenty or more.

The variety of mushrooms continued out in the lawns. Here I found more kinds, but just as much color as the forest growth. Usually, we do not see what the yard fungi is growing on, but beneath the surface is old decay wood from earlier days.

One mushroom of interest in the lawn is the milk mushroom. Also known by its scientific name of Lactarius, the mushroom gets its name from the white liquid, often called latex that will bleed from a cut on the surface. Caps of milk mushrooms will vary in size and color, but all have this characteristic milk bleeding as a sign of recognition. I have found that fresh specimen are more likely to bleed if cut with a knife. Cap and stem tissue are not as good at demonstrating this bleeding as are the gills (the thin "page-like" structures under the cap). The white latex is quick to appear on the gills surface after being cut.

Mushroom peak time is highly influenced by moisture, but with normal rainfall, we should continue to see much more fascinating fungi during our fall walks for the next several weeks.

SEPTEMBER
DAILY CLIMATE INFORMATION FOR DULUTH, MINNESOTA

Normal Records

DAY	AVERAGE HIGH	AVERAGE LOW	RECORD HIGH	RECORD LOW	SUNRISE	SUNSET
1	71	52	94/1894	30/1974	6:28	7:50
2	70	51	92/1983	34/1974	6:30	7:48
3	70	51	89/1960	32/1974	6:31	7:46
4	70	51	89/1897	36/1918	6:32	7:44
5	69	50	90/1947	34/1984*	6:33	7:43
6	69	50	91/1978	33/1986	6:35	7:41
7	69	50	95/1976	30/1986	6:36	7:39
8	68	49	92/1931	32/1956	6:37	7:37
9	68	49	90/1961*	33/1975	6:39	7:35
10	67	48	85/1908	31/1917	6:40	7:33
11	67	48	92/1931	31/1965	6:41	7:31
12	67	48	87/1948	29/2007	6:43	7:29
13	66	47	84/1990	30/1975*	6:44	7:27
14	66	47	84/1920	30/1964	6:45	7:25
15	65	46	89/1939	27/1964	6:46	7:23
16	65	46	89/1948	30/1959	6:48	7:21
17	65	46	90/1891	28/1959	6:49	7:19
18	64	45	84/2000*	29/1929	6:50	7:17
19	64	45	90/1984	27/1962	6:52	7:15
20	63	44	87/1891	23/1962	6:53	7:13
21	63	44	88/1908	28/1974	6:54	7:11
22	62	44	84/1922	23/1974	6:56	7:09
23	62	43	85/1891	28/1928	6:57	7:07
24	61	43	85/1892	26/2000	6:58	7:05
25	61	42	88/1920	25/1926	6:59	7:02
26	61	42	80/1923	23/1965	7:01	6:59
27	60	42	83/1987	27/1991	7:02	6:57
28	60	41	79/1956*	24/1961	7:03	6:55
29	59	41	83/1892	25/1984	7:05	6:53
30	59	40	82/1897	26/1972	7:06	6:51

*Denotes latest of multiple years
Average Temperature for September: 55.6 F
Average Precipitation for September: 4.11 inches
Average Snowfall for September: 0.1 inches

OCTOBER

O CTOBER GETS ITS NAME from the Latin word "octo" meaning "eight." October was the eighth month in the old Roman calendar that had ten months. With the addition of January and February, it became the tenth month.

BINAAKWE GIIZIS:
The Leaves-Falling Moon

PHENOLOGICAL NAMES:
The Leaf-Drop Month
The Month of Tamarack Color
The Month of First Freezings
The Month of Many Clear Days

OCTOBER HAS A COLORFUL BEGINNING with a dazzling show of foliage ending with a bare landscape of autumn. October sees frost on the grass in the morning, mild days, and chilly nights. Ice appears on ponds and sporadic snows become more numerous. October is football, World Series, corn and pumpkins. Occasionally we need jackets and furnaces often see the first use in months.

October is the next phase of color as aspen's yellow replaces the maple's red, replaced in turn as tamaracks give a golden glow from the wetlands. Late-blooming gentians blend with the fluffy seeds of fireweed and milkweed. Apples, acorns, rose hips, highbush cranberries, and mountain-ash ripen. Puffballs, oyster and scaly mushrooms hang onto trees as the last leaves fall. October often sees a forest scene of trees bare of leaves with no snow cover, allowing us to see the floor foliage of mosses, clubmoss, and ferns. These few weeks become a season of their own — AutWin.

We see migrating bald eagles, red-tailed and rough-legged hawks by day, while saw-whet owl movement abounds at night. This is the time of greatest diversity of sparrows in northland fields and woods and waterfowl numbers in wetlands. October is when we see preparation for the cold. Spiders balloon on clear afternoons, crane flies dance at dusk and late-season moths flit through chilly nights. Woolly bear caterpillars wander about, and hornets abandon their nests as the queen seeks a wintering site.

The last warblers, vireos, and thrushes and the first redpolls, snow bunting, and northern shrike are on the move. Squirrels and chipmunks fill our yards, deer check out the fields, and mice try to get into our houses.

Lingering cool clear days with plenty of color step towards the more somber time of ice and snow. October often has bright blue weather with colorful scenes that help us forget the passing summer with no regret.

OCTOBER HAPPENINGS: THE FROSTY LEAF-DROP MONTH

What to Look For:

EARLY OCTOBER
- peak of sparrow diversity
- arrival of Lapland longspurs
- migrant bluebirds
- ruffed grouse drumming
- migrant ducks
- red-bellied snakes moving to hibernation
- red meadowhawk dragonflies
- tree cickets
- ladybugs
- milbert's tortoiseshell butterflies
- daddy-long-legs
- phase II of tree color, aspens
- meadow mushrooms and beard fungi

MID OCTOBER
- red-tail hawk migration
- saw-whet owl migration
- coot migration
- loon grouping on lakes
- leafhoppers
- phase III of tree color, tamaracks
- pine needle colors
- peak of leaf drop
- scaly-cap mushrooms
- birdsnest and cup fungi

LATE OCTOBER
- first rough-legged hawks
- first northern shrike
- first snow buntings
- jumping mice and chipmunks moving to hibernate
- late frogs, turtles, snakes
- late-season moths
- woolly aphids
- crane fly swarms
- spider ballooning
- last of tree color, phase IV: weeping willows and silver maples
- red leaves of blackberries, blueberries and bunchberries

Sparrow Diversity of Early October

ARLY OCTOBER, WITH THE DAZZLING tree colors and mild temperatures, makes the northland a great place to be. Yellows and reds in every direction makes us come back for more, though we've seen this forest display before. But the arboreal show is only part of the autumn adventure.

Rains have given us fungal growth to see as well. And we'll see critters as they get ready for the coming cold. Some, such as late-season butterflies, ladybugs, snakes, turtles, frogs, and chipmunks, are seeking places to hibernate.

The bird migration has been active here since August. We saw a diverse and healthy movement of northern warblers as they flitted in the woods. Gradually, their numbers dropped. Now in early October, we see only the lingering yellow-rumped and palm warblers. Shorebirds have mostly gone, as have the large numbers of hawks. Broad-winged hawks numbered in the thousands in mid September at Hawk Ridge and, though the raptor flight will continue for weeks, such numbers will not be seen again this fall.

Other birds vying for our attention are the sparrows. Appearing to most people as ubiquitous little brown birds, sparrows are widely diverse and, what at first looks to be a lot of sameness proves to be quite an exciting group of birds to watch.

And there's no better time to see them than early October. An observant search through the region at this time can turn up as many as fifteen kinds, but for most of us, we'll be more likely to see ten species. Both the migrants from further north and our residents can be observed now. Northland breeding sparrows still with us are the spotted song sparrows, often seen in our yards and gardens, and its shy look-alike, the Lincoln sparrows, of the swamps and bogs. A scratching noise from a nearby woods may reveal another spotted sparrow. Red-brown fox sparrows regularly stop off here to feed on insects and worms on the forest floor before moving on in a couple of weeks. Chipping sparrows with their reddish crown and no streaks underneath nested in our yards. They're still here, but now are in flocks, frequently seen along roadsides. Also unstreaked below are swamp sparrows in the wetlands. Both will soon be joined by their northern twin, the tree sparrows.

Maybe the most abundant and easiest to see of the fall sparrow crowd is the white-throated sparrows. The birds carry a white throat patch, but also hold white lines above their head. Frequently, they'll come to our yards and feeders. Using binoculars, we can see that within the flocks are others. White-crowned sparrows have white above the head, but none on the throat. And on the largest of the sparrows, Harris sparrows, black hoods or chest markings are regular. Let's not forget a sparrow without a sparrow name. Juncos, sporting a gray coat and white side tail feathers, are expected visitors at our places now. Often the flocks are so active and common it is hard not to see them as we pass by.

The weather is sure to get colder and the migration will continue, but for now look out at the diverse visiting sparrows and enjoy them.

LINGERING ASTERS

In October, we get the autumn that's been growing more apparent each day.

The northland puts on quite a show at this time. We take time to look at the trees as their autumn glory fills them in color. Tall and green all summer, they stood amongst us, but we took little note. Now as they show us a blend of yellows, oranges, and reds, they demand our attention. It isn't often we make special trips to see foliage displays, but this is a regular part of the lives of many of us during the early part of this month. But the trees don't give all the color. The warmth of last month has delighted the roadsides with floral arrangements. Here we found the yellows of goldenrods, sunflowers, black-eyed susans, tansies, and evening primroses with whites of yarrows, fleabanes, daises, and asters. Another batch of asters now joins the thistles to add purple to the scene.

Now, with the chillier weather, frosts, and shorter days (darkness hours now exceed the light hours each day), most have succumbed. Blooming from early August until now, the plants appear to have accomplished their goals of seed formation, and most are now closing up for the season. But some hardy plants continue to bloom, the asters. Probably the most widespread and well-known of the fall flowers, they appear to be immune to the early autumn frosts. Their numerous blossoms of white and purple continue well into October.

Like many of these late-season flowers, asters are composites. This term means that their blossoms are composed of many small flowers. What most of us call a flower head is actually a cluster of many minute florets. The parts commonly referred to as petals are truly small flowers called ray flowers or rays. In the center, we see a circular part known as the disk. Like the surrounding rays, this disk is filled with many tiny flowers. With asters, rays surround the disk in numbers that vary from ten to fifty, and in our region they carry colors of white to pink to blue to purple. About ten kinds grow commonly in the northland's sunny fields, roadsides, and woods edges.

White ones include flat-top aster, marsh aster, calico aster, and heath aster while those of other colors are swamp aster, large-leaf aster, Lindley's aster, smooth aster, and New England aster. Ranging from a foot to four feet tall and in various habitats, the local asters all share the characteristic of abundant flowers that last late into fall. The name aster means star and may refer both to the blossoms that look like stars or the fact that the flower heads seem to be as numerous as the stars.

Keen observers have noticed their cold-weather persistence, and asters have been called other names such as fall-rose, frost flower, frostweed, good-bye summer, and Christmas daisy. A bit more specific is the name of Michaelmas daisy, which is a reference to the feast of St. Michael the archangel, September 29. Usually several kinds of our asters are still in bloom on this date, but eventually the frosts of fall are just a bit too tough for them, and they slowly succumb as colder temperatures of October move in. But for now, let's enjoy these last flowers of the season.

Golden Tamaracks in the Swamps

D**URING THE LAST WEEKS OF** S**EPTEMBER** and early weeks of October, the deciduous trees have demanded our attention. But like all performances, it comes to an end.

Rainy and windy days bring down thousands of leaves, and the woods, so colorful just the week before, now are open with a fresh layer of dried brown leaves on the ground. Even those trees whose leaves linger will soon surrender them to the winds of October. By mid month, the forest is nearly all bare, and the trees are ready to face the coming cold. Without leaves, they are able to conserve needed moisture throughout the arid days of winter, and snows break fewer branches.

But even with most trees bare, we can see trees still with leaves, some even green. These tend to be the evergreens or the nonnative trees growing in our midst. These late leafy ones, such as weeping willows, buckthorns, lilacs, and other yard trees, are from other parts of the world, but now grow here. Usually they are later to drop their leaves than our native trees. Lasting through late October or even mid November, these trees hold their leaves, but theirs will drop too. The exception are some red oaks, which hold their leaves through most of the winter.

Another spectacular show is just beginning now. At about the time our deciduous trees are through with their annual red-yellow spectacle, the tamaracks of the swamps make their move. Conifers of the wetlands, tamaracks (also called larch) have been holding green needles since last summer. Growing in the poor soils of such a habitat, the trees seldom grow large. Along with black spruce and a variety of wetland shrubs, they survive in these moist conditions, where many trees cannot. We usually pay them little attention.

But all that changes in mid October. For about two weeks, these conifers act like deciduous trees and put forth a dazzling yellow-gold color that gets the attention of all passersby. The northland has abundant swamps and bogs, and tamaracks thrive here. Driving in almost any direction will take us by such sites of this golden glow. It is as though these wetland trees are giving an encore to the earlier forest foliage display. Many say that tamaracks save the best show for last.

After this yellow-gold color, the trees continue to act like the broad-leaf trees and drop their leaves (needles). They also go through the winter devoid of leaves. Apparently, in this poor soil home, they need to hold water more than their upland cousins.

Arboreal colors will mostly be gone by late October, so now is a great time to visit some north country swamps and see this golden tamarack show.

WOOLLY APHIDS

LATE OCTOBER IN THE NORTHLAND is a remarkable time. The leaf drop earlier in the month has changed the landscape. For the next seven months, we will view the trees without their green foliage. At mid month, the tamaracks gave a finale to the colorful exit of the deciduous trees with a yellow-gold glow from the swamps. Now we look out, and into, an open woods. AutWin (a made-up name that I give to this time of year), the time between the leaf drop and the snow cover, is upon us. This amazing time is like a season all its own, unlike any other weeks of the year.

Only now with the trees devoid of leaves we see all the other greens of the forest. Mosses drape trunks, stumps, logs, and rocks continue their green attire, and we see just how common they are. Wood ferns and rock cap ferns also remain in their summer colors unlike other ferns. And clubmosses (cousins of ferns, not mosses) carpet the forest floor. These miniature evergreens also tell us of an unexpected abundance. But there is more.

While walking here at this time, I also notice the fungi, in the form of tough shelves sticking out from trees, and jellies and puffballs. And then there's that white stuff that looks like a fungus growth on alders. Alders are small trees, very common in the north country, mostly in the wetlands. Like other deciduous trees, these small woody plants dropped their leaves a few weeks ago, but unlike most, they did so without a colorful fanfare. Leaves were green and on branches one day, on the ground the next. When defoliated, the branches reveal happenings that were hidden during the warm leafy season. With many trees, hidden findings are nests of birds, squirrels, or hornets. But for some alders, a "long white growth" appears on the bare branches. This white pattern sure looks like a fungus growth. Closer inspection reveals numerous white strands projecting from a dark surface. They are easy to mistake for a fungus, but as I watch carefully, I see some movement. And I see that at the base of the white strands are a good number of dark bodies. This is a colony of insects, aphids, not fungi.

Known as woolly aphids, the colonies began in summer and settled into this site to feed on sap from the alder. With all the leaves gone, we can see them. Anyone gardening is well aware of aphids that gather on many plants, and seeing these tiny insects lined up on stems of late summer plants in not unusual. I have frequently watched their antics and movements on goldenrods during the warm days of August. Often ants stand by to guard them. Ants protect these aphid colonies that, in return for their protection, will provide their guardians with a sweet-tasting liquid, known as honey dew. Green, purple or dark, these familiar aphid groups fade with the cold.

But the woolly aphids continue into the fall. Perhaps their white coats that make them look like a fungus and so protect them from predation and will also help to keep these insects warmer. I'm not the only one to have discovered this late-season aphid colony and as I observe them, I see that they too are protected by ants. With other aphids gone, these white woollies are still producing honey dew. And ants still want this sweetness in these chilly days.

Autumn may linger for a few more weeks or a month, and I suspect that the alder will continue to host these white aphids until they drop to the ground for the winter, and slumber beneath a blanket of snow that is sure to come.

MILKWEED PODS IN FALL

LATE OCTOBER'S BLAND LANDSCAPE with trees devoid of leaves seems to fit in with the frequency of cloudy days we expect to see in November. Early snows may break this gray-brown scene, but these light coats are usually quick to melt. Not only do the woods look somber now, but so do the fields and roadsides. Here we see many dead-looking brown plants standing, most of which are holding fluffy material on the top. But there's more to be seen here.

Just as we discovered while walking in the forests during this autumn interlude, we find things to see in the open areas too. Goldenrods and asters that put on such a colorful show of yellow, purple, and white last month now are brown and reach up with the products of such blossoms. They are joined by several others, but maybe it is the milkweeds that put forth the biggest seeds.

Milkweed patches got more notice from passing insects than from us during the warm season, and bees, wasps, flies, moths, and butterflies all gathered on these fragrant plants. Many went for the rich nectar while others found the large leaves resourceful sites to feed and live even with its bitter white sap. The days passed with such activity and the flowers waned during late summer.

Replacing these odorous floral displays were green, oval-shaped pods. Loaded with seeds, they ripened during September and the outer covering of the pods turned gray. Dry autumn air caused the pods to split open, and the fluffy seeds burst forth. For the last month, milkweeds have had the white downy seeds extending from these holds. Often the first ones open in late September, but continue through the following weeks. Now, in late October, these seeds reach out as they wait for a breeze to disperse them. Any of us passing by such fields or roadsides can easily observe these large plants and the seed cluster. The green plant with large leaves and groups of pink flowers is only a memory. The gray stalk that we now see broadcasting its seeds to the winds looks little like that summer plant, but it is still quite noticeable.

211

Like other flowers out here in this autumn field such as gold-enrods and asters, milkweed seeds drift on the wind usually do not germinate. They are undeterred by such poor results, and grow back from hardy rootstocks that remain alive in subterranean homes.

We'll see these green plants and flowers here again next summer and the opening pods next fall.

Snakes Prepare for Cold

A S THE AUTUMN UNFOLDS from September into October, we continue to see how nature prepares for the coming cold. Probably the most obvious are the trees that shed their leaves after their blaze of color. If the trees were to retain their foliage, the same structures that provided food in the warmer time of the year will cause the plants to dry up in the cold. Wildflowers that bloomed in past weeks, took advantage of active insect pollinators, and now form seeds, using the winds of fall to disperse. Animals have other ways to meet the impending chill.

Basically, animals deal with winter in four ways. Migration to a warmer clime, usually seen among birds; hibernation, a strategy used by insects, reptiles, amphibians, and some mammals; death (after laying eggs), largely with insects, some spiders, a variety of annual plants, and others; and staying active, a condition mostly of birds and mammals. There are huge variations among each method of survival, and some do more than one. A good example of this last situation, as we may see in coming weeks, is ladybugs. Before cold-time dormancy, they migrate to a proper resting site and hibernate.

Another example of this I see regularly in early October is the behavior of snakes. Our two species of snakes common in the northland — the common garter and red-bellied — will hibernate for winter, but they choose a site, known as a hibernaculum, where they congregate and pass through the cold and dark. Sites are underground and in open cracks, pits, or such subterranean locales where they are able to go below the frost line. Though still cold in these places, snakes will survive with the help of snow as an insulating blanket.

A few years ago, during the winter of 2002-2003, the light snow cover and deep cold caused the death of many snakes as the frost penetrated deeper than their safety zone. The same winter saw the demise of huge numbers of frogs, especially spring peepers on the forest floor.

Though we may seldom see their hibernacula at this time in autumn, we can often watch these reptiles as they travel to find their

213

winter shelter. When I bike on the Willard Munger Trail during clear days in October, I not only look for traveling snakes, I *expect* to see them. Garter snakes are the larger of the two common varieties, and some females may reach up to two feet long. They are adorned with light-colored stripes on the body's length. The smaller red-bellied snake, usually less than one foot, is mostly brown above with the name-sake reddish-orange on the underside. Many locals refer to this small snake as "copper-belly." I find this term too easy to confuse with "copperhead," a type of poisonous snake found much further to the south. Our snake species are all harmless to us and don't need any more misconceptions or misunderstandings than already exist.

Feeding on a variety of small invertebrates, the snakes gather meals on their way to bed. Also, as they take the seasonal trek, they pause at warm places to bask. Most likely, that is part of the reason I see them on pavement now. Autumn nights and mornings are chilly, and it must feel good to them to warm a bit. These autumn days of October have a great deal to offer, and each day we can see a new story being acted out as northland nature copes with the coming cold in various ways.

MIGRANT BLUEBIRDS

The days of early October are full of new happenings, so much to note besides tree color. Due to recent rains, this has been a good mushroom time. Scaly pholiota are on trees with clusters of honey mushrooms at the stump's base. White meadow mushrooms arise in the lawns as well.

Among the birds, the migration continues. Raptors continue to pass over each day. Besides raptors, many songbirds are southing now too. On a recent morning, after a clear night, I saw flocks of juncos and their cousins, white-throated sparrows, in the yard. In the nearby woods are yellow-rumped warblers, kinglets, and groups of robins. And on utility wires along the roads, I saw good numbers of bluebirds.

Bluebirds, smaller cousins of robins, are regular migrants in the northland during the first half of October. Correctly known as eastern bluebirds (there are also western and mountain bluebirds), they are about eight inches long and though both males and females have a similar color pattern, males are darker. Blue on the head and back, white belly and a reddish throat and breast makes for a handsome bird. Their color along with pleasant warble songs and a diet of insects make bluebirds favorites for many. No surprise that they were chosen as state birds for two states (New York and Missouri).

Unlike other thrushes, bluebirds are cavity nesters. Hollow trees are suitable sites for their homes and they often take to bird houses. Birds thrive near open areas and frequent farms and fields where they find plenty of meals all summer.

Now, in October, the birds that returned here in April and scattered out to breed throughout the region are moving back to the south. Flocks are bigger now than those of spring. Young of the year are mixed with seasoned adults as they make this journey. Families gather and soon are joined by other familial units and groups number in the twenties and thirties. Usually we see these fall bluebirds sitting on roadside telephone lines and fences as we pass by. Though they do not sing as they did earlier in the season, it is not uncommon to hear their familiar warbles in calling to each other. These bluebird flocks will be with us for a few more weeks but with the cold, much of their food is gone and they must move on. Now is a good time to see this touch of blue added to the colorful October days.

MIGRANT SAW-WHET OWLS

THE REGULAR MIGRATION of raptors begun about mid August has been winding down. Huge numbers of birds moved through as summer became autumn. Large flocks of broad-winged hawks stole the show in September and, with rising thermals, their kettles numbered in the thousands during mid month. Wintering in Central America, the broad-wings have a long way to go, and these mid-sized buteos are now far to the south.

We tend to forget the hawk migration after the big days have passed, but now in October, the visitors to Hawk Ridge are still treated to the sight of many large birds, especially red-tailed hawks. With cooler winds and temperatures, watching may be a bit uncomfortable, but the flight continues and October and November days often give great views of rough-legged hawks, goshawks, bald eagles, and perhaps even some golden eagles. The raptor migration time here is from mid August to late November, about one hundred days.

The passing hawks, eagles, vultures, ospreys, and kestrels are just those that fly by in the daytime. Another flight of migratory raptors happens at night, the owls. A diligent search of the northland can reveal about ten kinds of owls each year. The most common ones are permanent residents—great horned owls and barred owls. Others come to us only in winter—snowy owls, great gray owls, hawk owls, and boreal owls. Those mostly known from migration, though records of nesting and wintering can be found among them, are the long-eared owls, short-eared owls, saw-whet owls, and maybe a screech owl. This time of October is an active time for these migrants.

The medium-sized long-eared and short-eared owls are seldom seen or heard in their southern flight, but the tiny saw-whets are more likely to be noted. Only about six or seven inches long, saw-whets could fit in your hand. Owls are in two groups when it comes to "ear tufts." Great horned, long-eared, short-eared, and screech owls all have the feather tufts sticking up, but the rest of the north country owls, including the diminutive saw-whets, do not have these.

Saw-whet owls may breed here and some winter here, but the bulk are migratory and pass through. And now is the time. Moving from a boreal forest summer home, they winter further to the south. Sometimes, nights in October can be quite active with their movements. Banders at Hawk Ridge have reported more than one hundred in a single night at this time on several years.

Though most of us are not likely to catch them, there are three other ways that we may know of their presence. Some will give their namesake call as they travel. Named by lumberjacks who thought the sound was like that of a saw being sharpened, most of us are more likely to compare it to the beeping noise of a backing truck. Flying low, maybe three of four feet above the ground, many have unfortunately been hit by cars. It is all too common to find the bodies of such mishaps the next day. And finally, sometimes chickadees will locate a roosting owl and surround it with harassing calls, thus alerting us to their presence.

OCTOBER
Daily Climate Information for Duluth, Minnesota

Normal Records

Day	Average High	Average Low	Record High	Record Low	Sunrise	Sunset
1	58	40	80/1989*	20/1961	7:07	6:49
2	58	40	86/1953	17/1961	7:09	6:47
3	57	39	77/1913*	22/1999	7:10	6:45
4	57	39	83/1922	22/1952	7:11	6:43
5	57	39	84/1963	21/1988*	7:13	6:41
6	56	38	83/1961	23/1935	7:14	6:39
7	56	38	80/2010*	24/2001	7:16	6:37
8	55	37	82/1943	24/1989*	7:17	6:35
9	55	37	76/1960*	20/1972	7:18	6:33
10	54	37	82/1938	18/1906	7:20	6:31
11	54	36	79/1995	21/1936*	7:21	6:29
12	53	36	81/1995	18/1988	7:22	6:28
13	53	36	80/1956	19/1917	7:24	6:26
14	53	36	80/1947	21/1978	7:25	6:24
15	52	35	82/1929	21/1952	7:27	6:22
16	52	35	81/1953	16/1952	7:28	6:20
17	51	35	80/1961	12/1952	7:29	6:18
18	51	34	79/1945	16/1972	7:31	6:17
19	50	34	78/1884	12/1972	7:32	6:15
20	50	34	79/1953	16/1952	7:34	6:13
21	49	33	80/1901	14/1913	7:35	6:11
22	49	33	76/1901	9/1936	7:37	6:10
23	48	33	78/1963	9/1936	7:38	6:08
24	48	32	71/1998	12/1887	7:39	6:06
25	47	32	72/1989	8/1887	7:41	6:05
26	47	32	75/1989	10/1936	7:42	6:03
27	46	31	70/1966	6/1917	7:44	6:01
28	46	31	66/1948	12/1905	7:45	6:00
29	45	30	74/1937	13/1925	7:47	5:58
30	45	30	73/1901	8/1925	7:48	5:56
31	44	30	74/1950	8/1878	7:50	5:55

Denotes latest of multiple years
Average Temperature for October: 43.2 F
Average Precipitation for October: 2.85 inches
Average Snowfall for October: 2.3 inches

NOVEMBER

NOVEMBER GETS ITS NAME from the Latin word "novem" meaning "nine." November was the ninth month in the old Roman calendar that had ten months. With the addition of January and February, it became the eleventh month.

GASHKADINO GIIZIS:
The Ice-Forming Moon

PHENOLOGICAL NAMES:
The Month of Lakes Freezing
The Cloudy Month
The Month of Deer Rut

NOVEMBER IS THE CLOUDY freeze-up month. Ponds reluctantly take on a new ice cover, and by late month, lakes join them in wearing this chilly coat. November sees the return of snow and after some melting, it remains on the frozen ground. Northern fronts slowly reintroduce us to subzero as the month wanes.

November's wet snow tells of the coming winter. Each day we read what the animal tracks are telling us of their activities in the autumn chill. Snow replaces rain, coats replace jackets, skis replacing bikes, and ice fishing huts replacing boats.

Evergreen ferns, mosses, and clubmosses on the forest floor among the bare trees are easy to see before being covered by the ever-increasing snow blanket.

Redpolls and pine grosbeaks joining chickadees, nuthatches, woodpeckers, and squirrels at feeders while visiting tree sparrows, juncos, and snow buntings move further south. Lingering migrants — bald eagle, rough-legged hawks, and goshawks — continue their way south as freezing wetlands send snow geese and swans on as well.

We get our last view of a chipmunk as it goes to its winter den while the deer mouse tries to move into ours. Flying squirrels give squeaking calls as they move among the branches on these long nights. Beavers build a greater cache as ice closes in above them. The bear takes it last meals of roots, fruits, and small game before wandering off to sleep. Deer hunters seek the ten-point buck as the white-coated snowshoe hare scampers off.

November is us giving thanks for the harvest, the wood pile, and the warm home in preparation for the coming cold.

November Happenings: The Cloudy Freeze-Up Month

What to Look For:

Early November
- migrant snow buntings, pine siskins, tree sparrows
- first redpolls
- long-eared, short-eared owls
- moles and shrews
- woollybear caterpillars
- clubmosses and mosses
- wood ferns
- British soldier and reindeer lichens
- horsetails
- milkweed seed pods
- puffballs

Mid November
- rough-legged hawks
- deer mice
- deer rut
- beavers caching near lodges
- buckthorns dropping green leaves
- rose hips
- sumac berries
- highbush cranberries and hawthorns
- goldenrod and aster seeds
- mullien and primrose rosettes
- jelly fungi

Late November
- bald eagles
- flying squirrels at feeders
- otters in freezing lakes
- tracks in early snow
- winter berry holly
- burdock seeds
- turkey tail fungi

WILD ASPARAGUS

SEEING NOVEMBER'S RATHER DRAB SCENE upon us now, it is a bit hard to think that just a few weeks ago, we delighted in the colors of October. Most of this foliage dropped at about mid month from broadleaf trees. The tamaracks followed with their golden glow encore and also exited. Browns and grays make up more of the landscape as we move through November. But some of the plants still hang on to color.

Red leaves can be seen in the bushes and small plants. Several still hold their bright colors. Checking the sides of roads and trails now, I see raspberries, blackberries, blueberries, bunchberries, and roses still with leaves varying from scarlet to burgundy. A few trees linger with yellow, and commuters will note the colorful leaves of willows (including weeping willow), silver maples, cottonwoods, and lilacs. Some of the trees of yards, parks, and cities have lasted longer. And there are a couple of plants are completely yellow in this less-than-colorful scene. A strange pair now gives us roadside light. One is a grass while the other is an escaped garden plant.

A common, though non-native, grass in the northland, reed canary grass, now stands with golden blades in abundance. One can drive for long distances and continue to view this plant in its autumn attire. And now is also the time of the yellow-gold asparagus.

Most of us think of asparagus as a garden plant or merely a vegetable for dinner that satisfies only a few. Plants indeed grow in gardens and, as a perennial, will come back each year once established. Those of us who know such patches are willing return each spring to sample the new juicy shoots, quite delicious. The wild plant that we now see is the same species.

Back in the 1960s, author Euell Gibbons wrote a book about eating wild edibles. Though the book dealt with more than forty wild foods, he decided to title it *Stalking the Wild Asparagus*. He wisely chose a plant well known as a garden plant but, as an escapee, now common along roadsides and as it is the same as the tame plant, safe to eat.

Plants grow through mid summer and reach a bush-like shape up to three or four feet tall. They put out many branches with very thin leaves and tiny flowers. Most of us do not even see the flowers, but plants get pollinated and the numerous seeds are able to scatter through the countryside leading to this wild state we see today.

They stand out here tall and green all summer, almost invisible amid the wealth of greenery available, and we go by without much of a second glance. Even as the asparagus turned yellow in October, we did not notice them much, but now as the colors continue into November, at a time when most else has faded, we take note. Many a passerby will wonder what this yellowish bush along the highway is and where it come from.

Even if we don't like the taste of asparagus as a vegetable, we can appreciate the visual treat on our route during these November days. Though their colors linger, they will fade with the coming chill.

WOOLYBEAR CATERPILLARS

PASSING FROM OCTOBER INTO NOVEMBER, we say goodbye to much of nearby nature that has been with us for months. The most obvious are the leaves on the trees and the hardy wild flowers that have lasted this long. We also see the last of the turtles, snakes and frogs as they slip into protected sites to cope with the cold. Many of the birds have moved on. We have probably seen our last warbler and nearly all of the robins are gone.

Departing too are the local insects. This abundant and diverse group is so common due to their being able to adapt and cope with various environmental conditions. When it comes to dealing with winter, they run the gamut. Some insects—the best known being the monarch butterflies—migrate. Others will hibernate, going dormant, until next spring. We see this with some butterflies (mourning cloaks), ladybugs, and leafhoppers. Many feel the impending cold and respond by laying eggs and dying. Grasshoppers are notable, but this group abounds. And even a few insects remain active all winter. Most are tiny and stay hidden under the forest leaf litter and snowpack and usually not seen.

An interesting one that we do see now is the caterpillar most of us refer to as the "woolybear" because of its hair-covered body. About one to two inches long with stiff hair colored black and orange-brown, the critter is easy not to see. However, since they are so active during the autumn, often extending through October and into November, we do see them. When among the leaves and plants of the forest floor, they remain inconspicuous, but when crossing roads, trails, and sidewalks, these caterpillars are often found.

Any time we have mild temperatures, even without sunlight, I expect to see these moth larvae as they scurry across our paths heading for a goal all their own. Unlike many moths that winter in the cocoon stage, this moth spends the winter as a curled up caterpillar. They are able to withstand the cold of the northland with just leaves or other debris as a protection. Next spring, we'll witness their movements again when they wake and form cocoons.

Woolybears are seen and recognized by most of us, but few know the adult form of this moth. The young will mature as a yellow-orange moth in June and July. Known as Isabella tiger moths, they fly at night and are much less likely to be seen when grown.

The hairy body of the woolybear has even led to a story of the critter's ability to predict the coming winter. Black hairs are on both ends of the body with orange-brown in the middle. Some say that the more black they have, the colder the winter will be. Some swear it is the middle brown that predicts the length of winter. As they have a somewhat random percentage of black and brown in a variety of individuals, a few might seem to get it right.

As the caterpillars grow, they molt and each new coat gives a bit more black, the older ones are blacker. Let's not ask these caterpillars about the winter, but let's just enjoy them before they are asleep in their snow-covered sites.

RUSTY BLACKBIRDS

During October, the bird migration was continuous. Raptors were common with plenty of ducks, and geese as well. Migrant songbirds in successive waves left the north. During the waning days of the month, migrant flocks include tree sparrows, longspurs, some early snow buntings and the often noisy, but always hungry blackbirds.

Several times in the last few weeks, I observed groups of these medium size dark birds in trees, usually by roads and frequently near cornfields. I didn't always see the birds first, but instead they were located by their loud calling and singing in a cacophony of voices and tunes.

At first glance, the flocks seem to be all the same kind of bird, but on closer look, I found four kinds. The blended blackbird flocks include grackles, red-winged blackbirds, Brewer's blackbirds, and rusty blackbirds. All are dark in color though females are often browner and, in the fall, rusty blackbirds live up to their name with their rust-colored plumage. They are the only one of the four not a resident of the region. Rusties nest in Canada. Grackles often make up the greatest numbers of the group with red-wings vying for a tight second place. The other two are in smaller numbers.

It is not unusual to have one hundred or more in these noisy flocks. Like many birds at this time, they are heading to their wintering site—for them states to the south. Stopping off for a meal along the way may keep them occupied for several days or a week if they find a treat of ripe corn. Flocks are noisy on these fall days. Among the squeaks and chips, we can sometimes hear the spring songs of the birds. Rusties, however, tend to be more silent.

About nine inches long, rusty blackbirds are all brown with some belly streaks and yellow eyes. Males wear a black color in spring. I rarely see them migrate before October. But once they start to arrive, they may be part or entirely in flocks that we see along the roadsides. Many a commuter on chilly November mornings has seen large flocks of blackbirds that stretch out as they fly over the highway as we pass by.

Blackbirds devour seeds (including occasional visits to bird feeders), but will take to wetlands and fields to gather insects and other invertebrates as well. Their appetite for corn has gotten them in trouble at times, but by November, much of this crop has been harvested.

Blackbirds wintering in the northland are extremely unusual ,and soon they will be moving on. These flocks that group and call in early November will not be here by the end of the month. We will not hear their noisy songs until next March or April. Let's enjoy watching and listening to them now.

SMALL MAMMALS PREPARE FOR THE COMING COLD

L IKE IT OR NOT, BY THE TIME we get into November, the chill is beginning to move in, and we have more darkness each day. Frost is expected and ponds often show a coat of ice each morning. We are still far from the cold that we call winter, but each day we take another step in that direction. We, along with the rest of nature, are preparing for this time in a variety of ways. Trees shed their leaves in anticipation of the arid air that prevails in winter. Those small plants with evergreen leaves tend to be low and close to the ground and so will be protected by the coming snowpack.

Insects have mostly ceased their activity, as have the spiders. Birds migrate and form plumages that give protection to their winter lives. Fortunately for us, we have a number of resident birds that will remain and provide plenty of cold-weather enjoyment. Small mammals show quite a diversity as they get ready for this change of seasons.

Cold survival comes in four options: migrate, hibernate, die or remain active (often with behavioral adaptations). Among our small mammal population, we see three of these four. Migration only happens with bats, which leave often at night, and so we are not likely to see this behavior. Those that remain active are very easy to observe now and probably no day goes by that we don't see gray or red squirrels getting material for winter caches. And maybe we note how deer mice are getting into our houses and cabins as they disperse to find a good wintering site.

We have several small mammals that do what we call hibernate. This torpid state varies with different ones that use this method. Perhaps skunks and raccoons are least likely to be considered hibernators. They sleep through much of the cold, but are out and about when mild days occur in winter. Resident bats and chipmunks go into a deeper slumber, but they do wake with some movement, usually without going outside their den during the dark months. These waking periods explain why chipmunks are so active in October gathering and storing food for snacking in the cold times.

Deepest sleepers and true hibernators are best seen in three local small mammals: jumping mice (small mice with large hind legs and an extremely long tail) and three ground squirrels: woodchucks (groundhogs), Franklin ground squirrels, and the thirteen-lined ground squirrel. None of three rodents are abundant in the region though each has sites where they are likely to be found. Each prepares for this extreme dormant stage by eating much in these days of autumn. Dining on seeds and plants, they put on weight as quickly as possible and may actually double their mass at this time.

Within the safety of a subterranean den, they curl into a comfortable position and begin a doze that will last until next April. Heartbeat and breathing rates drop to the minimal, and the body temperature lowers. Despite this apparently easy and safe way of dealing with winter, hibernators don't all survive. But now as we enter November, we marvel at how they and all of nature prepares for this coming cold season.

A Visit to a Beaver Pond

ONCE WE REACH MID NOVEMBER, we enter the time of change. During these weeks in the second half of the month, we see landscape alterations that will persist all winter. During the last six weeks, the ground has been covered by the fallen leaves. Scattered sporadic snowfalls have given a white dusting, but usually these early snows come and go. Only as we exit the month is the blanket of white more likely to continue, thanks to the frozen ground.

Similarly, the wetlands show changes. As temperatures regular dip below freezing, more of the ponds get covered with ice, and cooler days means it doesn't all melt before night and more ice formation. Soon they are frozen over. They are joined by the shallow swamps and finally, usually after the 20th of November, lakes also freeze, from smallest to largest.

This year, November began very mild, but we felt the usual chill by mid month. Many area lakes were covered by ice on the 18th, compared to the 23rd for 2007. Each year is different.

It is always interesting to watch the local wildlife deal with the cold. Hibernators, like frogs, are no longer with us. Even most of the migrants are gone. The ones that we see now are likely to stay throughout the cold and remain active. The pond I visit looks much the same as others near here. It is coated with ice and has a little snow around the bank. Ice is strong enough to support me, and I walk around the entire pond, staying along the edge. I break through only once during my journey.

The beaver lodge stands large and strong as it was when I came here before the freeze up. All is silent now,and I see none of the beaver family that lives here. But I do see several signs of the presence of these big rodents and their preparation for winter.

On the shore are several recently downed trees with the telltale tooth marks of the beavers. Branches have been dragged off to the water, many of which have bark removed. New branches and sticks from these trees are on the lodge, adding more strength and insulation to the wooden frame.

Out in the water near the lodge is a large gathering of sticks and twigs. This seemingly random arrangement will provide the winter food supply. Much of the cache is frozen in the ice, but enough is available for the beavers to reach under water to carry them through the cold times. Near the lodge, I see a site where the ice has been kept open. Apparently, the beavers push through the frozen cover for some movement above before it becomes too thick.

It looks as though the beavers are settled into the den with a nearby stash of food for the impending winter.

TURKEY-TAIL FUNGI

L ate November is a time we see nature settling in for the coming cold. Most of our songbirds have gone. Further south, they will be better able to find food and shelter to cope. Many of those staying with us through the coming season are the resident birds that change to a diet of seeds and berries. Chickadees, nuthatches, blue jays, and woodpeckers all do well here. Others wintering with us come from the north. For pine grosbeaks, redpolls, snow buntings, and Bohemian waxwings, this is south.

Hibernating mammals, reptiles, amphibians and insects have begun their long sleep. Any still out now are gathering bedtime snacks and will not be seen much more, even on the milder days. We usually think of animals as preparing for winter, but so do plants.

Deciduous trees dropped their leaves and are now ready for the cold. During the arid days of winter, broadleaf trees would dehydrate if they kept their leaves. Conifers with their thin leaves (needles) are able to cope with winter better by remaining foliated.

Some plants of the forest floor—mosses, clubmosses, and a few flowering plants such as wintergreen, hepatica, and pyrola—will remain green all winter. They use the dead leaf cover along with the snowpack as protection from the deepest cold.

Fungi will usually not grow in winter. Darkness does not slow fungi much, but cold and dryness do. Mushroom season is well past, and they will not be seen again until the wet warmth of spring.

The diverse fungi do have some that remain visible. Those are easy to see now and through the coming cold, even though they are not growing. Best known of these winter fungi are the shelf fungi. Also known as bracket fungi, their growths stick out from tree trunks and stumps in a flat shape parallel to the ground. Many kinds exist here in the northland. Some are specific to certain trees, such as birch and conifers. Others will grow on nearly any available site.

One such fungus is called turkey-tail. This unusual name refers to the concentric circles and color patterns seen on the top side. The fungus may grow near the ground on a sawed stump or higher on a tree trunk, but always on the same plane as the forest floor.

Some shelf fungi grow for many years and become hard as wood. Not so with the turkey-tail. Even though it is perennial and may be seen all winter and more to come, it is quite flexible.

Turkey-tail fungus, clustered in five- to ten-inch growths, provides for a pleasant sight for anyone taking a stroll in the late November woods.

SNOW BUNTINGS OF NOVEMBER

As usual, the month of November shows its two sides. We often begin with mild temperatures and though the month is often called "gray November," being typically the cloudiest month of the year, we marveled when we get clear dry days. But then, as we approach mid month, we see a different view of the month. Whereas the first half of November gives us an average reading of nearly forty degrees, the second half drops to the twenties. And with the chill, we deal with a significant snowfall and subsequent freezing of the ground. The bare ground during the early days has become blanketed with snow as we exit the month. Icing is seen in ponds, swamps, and lakes. The continuing freeze-up gives a completely different look to the woods and wetlands than thirty days ago.

Not only do we have a change in the weather, but also quite a variation with the migrants as well. Sparrows, juncos, tree sparrows, and fox sparrows that arrived earlier in the fall left us during the first week of November. Their absence was quickly filled by a few more northern Canada birds that moved this way. About mid month, I observed flocks of redpolls, Bohemian waxwings, and pine grosbeaks in the woods while a scattering of rough-legged hawks began to appear along the roadsides. Out in open water, goldeneyes swam and one evening at dusk, and I heard and then saw a flock of about fifty tundra swans. (This is not unusual to see in spring, but a bit so in fall.) But the abundant southbound migrant as we began the month of November was the snow buntings.

Another species of sparrows, snow buntings appear to be appropriately named, and frequently they are seen in snowy scenes. Breeding in the tundra, they are at home in open spaces. Here, despite the cold and wind often felt at such sites, they do quite well. A typical view of these small birds (about seven inches) is a flock flying up from the roadsides and field edge. Most of the groups I saw this month were twenty to fifty birds, but I have seen flocks that numbered in the hundreds as they feed on seeds out in the chilly fields of the northland.

During summer, snow buntings are mostly white, but by the time that we see them in fall, they have changed into a cryptic outfit of brown on the back and white below. Scattered in the open fields, they are able to move and gather seeds without attracting much attention. When taking wing, they reveal large white wing patches that make them easy to identify when in flight. We can see why they are sometimes called "snowflakes" or said to be drifting like "leaves in the wind." Recently as I walked a road, I observed a few of these snow birds in front of me at the edge. I thought I saw maybe five taking a meal, but when scared up, I counted twenty! Their feathers camouflaged them so well in this field setting.

As the cold and snow move in, many of these field birds move on, mostly wintering in open country south of here. But I still see some flocks now and usually snow buntings are with us through much of December. And they will continue to impress us with how well they are able to cope with the bleak conditions of the fields. Those leaving will stop by here again as they head north in the spring.

FLYING SQUIRRELS

MANY HOURS OF THESE NOVEMBER days are regularly spent watching bird feeders. We enjoy seeing the birds as they get close to the house in their feeding activities each day. Though they often gorge themselves with seeds, these feeder birds can do very well without our handouts.

Each day the well-loved black-capped chickadees, red- and white-breasted nuthatches join downy and hairy woodpeckers to dine just beyond our house. These five kinds occasionally share their site with blue jays, red-bellied woodpeckers, and finches, usually goldfinches, but the flocks could include pine siskins, redpolls, or pine grosbeaks. During these days of short daylight between the late sunrises and early sunsets, there is almost no time that does not have some activity from the feeding birds.

And they are not the only ones to get well fed here. Gray squirrels are quick to locate free meals on the feeders as well. Agile and arboreal as they are, the grays climb and jump to gain access to nearly any feeding sites. Those not bothering to come up on the feeders find plenty of spilled seeds on the ground. Each day, except for the very cold or snowy ones, squirrels gather in large numbers. Their smaller cousins, the red squirrels, come by too. Not as big as grays, the reds are very aggressive. It is not unusual for them to scare off their larger cousins.

Feeder activity continues from dawn to dusk, but I have found in recent years that it continues after dark. After sunset, the next batch of hungry neighbors moves in. We keep the feeder lighted so we can look out on nocturnal flying squirrels that descend from higher up in trees to get their meals while many also glide in from other trees. Occasionally, we may even hear their squeaking noises in the trees at this time.

Even smaller than the red squirrels, flyers are only about five or six inches long with a big flat tail. This tail acts as a rudder as they leap between trees. During such flights (actually glides) they stretch out their front and back legs to form a gliding membrane. Maneuvering through the trees at night takes a good deal of agility and skill. Like many other nocturnal mammals, flying squirrels have large eyes. These eyes, along with their soft fur and the fact that we can get quite close to them, makes these night-active squirrels favorites with many people. Observing them on feeders, they do look cute, and provide us with much entertaining winter wildlife watching, but those having these small mammals living in their house find them a bit less attractive.

Like the other squirrels and birds, flying squirrels can do very well through the winter without us, but they provide companionship and make our long dark nights a lot more interesting.

NOVEMBER
Daily Climate Information for Duluth, Minnesota

Normal Records

Day	Average High	Average Low	Record High	Record Low	Sunrise	Sunset
1	44	29	68/1990	2/1951	6/7:51	4/5:53
2	43	29	71/1903	-1/1951	6/7:53	4/5:52
3	43	28	73/1903	2/1951	6/7:54	4/5:50
4	42	28	69/1975	4/1991*	6/7:56	4/5:49
5	42	27	68/1975	6/1951	6/7:57	4/5:48
6	41	27	66/1916	-1/1991	6/7:58	4/5:46
7	40	27	65/1874	-1/1991	6/7:59	4/5:45
8	40	26	69/1999	-5/2003	7:01	4:44
9	39	26	71/1999	5/1959	7:03	4:42
10	39	25	64/1917	1/1986	7:04	4:41
11	38	25	62/1930	-3/1986	7:06	4:40
12	38	24	60/1884	-6/1966	7:07	4:38
13	37	23	67/1999	-7/1986	7:09	4:37
14	36	23	63/1953	-3/1959*	7:10	4:36
15	36	22	64/1939	-4/1933*	7:12	4:35
16	35	22	64/1931	-10/1933	7:13	4:34
17	35	21	68/1953	-9/1959	7:15	4:33
18	34	21	64/1904	-4/1932	7:16	4:32
19	34	20	55/1912	-10/1932	7:17	4:31
20	33	20	61/1925	-11/1921	7:19	4:30
21	32	19	64/1990	-13/1880	7:20	4:29
22	32	18	52/2006*	-9/1880	7:21	4:28
23	31	18	51/1907	-10/1956	7:23	4:28
24	31	17	53/1984*	-17/1884	7:24	4:27
25	30	17	53/1913	-16/1985	7:26	4:26
26	30	16	55/1960*	-9/1977	7:27	4:25
27	29	16	60/1998	-12/1985	7:28	4:25
28	29	15	49/1899*	-16/1875	7:29	4:24
29	28	15	53/1932	-29/1875	7:31	4:24
30	28	14	52/1962	-23/1964	7:32	4:23

*Denotes latest of multiple years
Average Temperature for November: 28.8 F
Average Precipitation for November: 2.09 inches
Average Snowfall for November: 13.7 inches

DECEMBER

DECEMBER GETS ITS NAME from the Latin word "decem" meaning "ten." December was the tenth month in the old Roman calendar that had ten months. With the addition of January and February, it became the twelfth month.

MANIDOO GIIZISOONS:
The Little Spirit Moon

PHENOLOGICAL NAMES:
The Dark Month
The Month of Rivers Freezing
The Month of the Winter Solstice

ECEMBER IS THE YEAR AT ITS DARKEST. A lethargic sun appears late and sleeps early. But the eight hours of daylight give way to bright nights when the full moon reflects off new snow. December has clear dark nights that perform the geminid meteor shower at mid month. We watch the show while our feet are freezing.

December has the winter solstice. We note the days of short daylight and slow reversal that will bring longer days. And we celebrate the holidays. December sees dry snows taking the place of the earlier wet ones. By early December, sub-zero becomes common and the snow cover is here to stay. Area lakes hold new snows and ice huts while the nearby woods is littered with animal tracks and ski trails. And rivers reluctantly also wear a sheet of ice. Porcupines go for arboreal meals, squirrels locate caches from last fall, mice go under the snow, and chipmunks go to sleep. The hopping tracks of white-coated hare and ermine are seen in the woods, and deer, foxes, and raccoons walk through the fields and yards. December has an occasional mild day that reveals insect and spider activity on the snow.

Full feeders draw nuthatches, blue jays, woodpeckers, and grosbeaks along with the ever-present chickadees and squirrels. Winter owls and hawks appear in our neighborhood during their hungry hunts. December sees us sitting back in our warmth to watch this critter show.

Evergreens now draped in holiday attire cope with the cold in their own way. Green pines, spruces, cedars, and balsam stand in the serene landscape, and we see just how common they are.

December is the start of serious winter as deepening snows sends deer to yard up, skunks and raccoons to nap, and mink, martens, and foxes to hunt beyond their usual time and place. But late December is also a time of change as the days very slowly lengthen and the coyote start marking territorial sites in anticipation of a cold breeding season.

December Happenings: The Dark Month

What to Look For:

Early December
- golden-crowned kinglets
- pine grosbeaks
- nuthatches, goldfinches, jay at feeders
- white ermine and snowshoe hare
- winter crane flies, wolf spiders on snow
- winterberry holly in the swamps
- crab apples and mountain-ash berries
- shelf fungi

Mid December
- snowy owls
- pileated woodpeckers
- goldeneyes in open water
- otters on ice
- minks and pine martens
- vole holes in snow
- red oaks, ironwoods with brown leaves
- black knot fungi

Late December
- goldfinch flocks at feeders
- great gray owls
- porcupines
- coyotes
- moose
- spruces, balsams
- cedars and hemlocks
- green rock cap ferns
- dwarf mistletoes in conifers

EARLY-SEASON TRACKS

NOVEMBER TYPICALLY GIVES US LITTLE LASTING SNOW. The sporadic snow showers that occurred several times in the second half of the month may total just a few inches. What we did receive mostly melted on many surfaces. Cold consistently below freezing caused lots of these substrates to be frosted before wearing a snow coat. As we exited the month, we were able to look out on a light covering, in some places only a dusting. Such snows leave much to be desired for snowmobile and ski enthusiasts, but at some places, it does set the scene for some good animal tracking.

On a recent walk in the woods, I noticed how the snow that had fallen on the leaf litter was melted, but that which landed on downed logs was still there. Apparently, enough geothermal heat was able to melt snow on the dead leaves, but the logs were too cold. Indeed, snow falling on most surfaces was gone the next day. However, there are places that I find snow lasting — the iced over bodies of water. As we move into December this will only build.

The cold slick ice of ponds and lakes holds the snowfall that melted elsewhere. And these sites, sometimes quite large, are excellent locales for finding animal tracks early in the season. Snow of not more than an inch deep allows for easy animal movement. The extreme cold has not yet hit us, and plenty of critters still move about in such a setting, often at night.

I'm never disappointed in the tracks discovered in swamps. Each day, I read the stories written by deer, fox, coyote, rabbit, hare, squirrel, raccoon, skunk, weasel, mink, shrew, and mouse. They tell of their searches for meals and shelters. They reveal how many were active here, how long ago, and what direction they went. And every time I come here, I find new tracks that tell me of more happenings. With the exception of deer and squirrels, I seldom see the track makers, but this evidence of their presence adds much to the scene.

Snow on lakes is often affected by wind. Frequently tracks here are covered. I find swamps are more protected and in among the growth of reeds and cattails, many mammals are active. It takes a little practice to recognize who was here, but different footprints and gaits show much about their identity.

Most of these mammals move on their toes. These include members of the dog family, cat family, weasel family and most rodents. Deer and moose are animals that actually walk on their toe nails (hoofs). Only a few go about on the whole foot, most notable are raccoon and bear. With bears asleep in December, raccoons are the ones that leave footprints showing toe marks, but also a heel. They waddle over many of our home sites since they do well in cities, but their tracks are often seen in the snow-covered wetlands as well. The ice below appears dark and the tracks can be easily discerned.

Deeper snows will soon change the scene, but for now, a walk over the snow-covered ice reveals many signs of the other wildlife wintering with us.

CONIFERS PROVIDE WINTER BEAUTY AND SHELTER

THOUGH MANY OF US NOW LOOK for and take home an evergreen tree for the holidays, we really don't need this annual celebration to make note of conifers. With a landscape of snow and bare broadleaf trees, the green trees stand out. Our forests are mixed, and both the conifer and deciduous woody plants grow here all year.

Now and through the rest of the winter we see just how common evergreens are in the region. Not only do they stand out more in December, the evergreens also hold more snow on their branches. Indeed, snow-ladened spruces and pines make up many of our season greeting cards.

The northland is home to ten native conifer trees with others that have been introduced. Native pines include red (Norway), white, and jack pines. Spruces are represented by two kinds, the black of the wetlands and the white from the uplands. White cedars grow in swamps, while balsams are scattered through the mixed forests. A couple of short trees, almost bushes, grow in the area too. Both, the low junipers and yews, grow no more that a few feet tall. In the wetlands are the coniferous tamaracks, our only conifer that drops its needles each fall — evergreens that are not ever green, a deciduous conifer. Another one, the hemlock, is rare in Minnesota but common in some northern Wisconsin woods.

Not only are evergreens easy to see now, they also provide much for the wintering wildlife. Cones of pines and spruces open in the dry winter air, allowing for seeds to be sampled by several birds — crossbills, nuthatches, and jays — along with the ever-present red squirrels. Many birds take shelter among the tightly packed needled branches. Lots of winter nights are spent in such hiding places. And these refuges often extend down from the trees to the ground (especially with spruces). Here the bent down branches covered with snow touch the snowpack and create protected chambers.

Since the snowfalls of early December, I have noticed many tracks of rabbits, hare, squirrels, and deer mice going into such sites.

Here too, chickadees, nuthatches, and cardinals go from bird feeders to settle down for their snacks of sunflower seeds. And ruffed grouse sneak into the bases of trees to hide as well.

The conifer with thin leaves, what we call needles, are well adapted to life in the cold and, unlike the leaves of the deciduous trees, they can hold them all winter. Thin needles provide for less evaporation and remain intact for the entire cold season.

No doubt, evergreens give plenty of beauty to the winter scene and they are a holiday favorite of ours, but the coniferous trees of the northland also use their great adaptations to survive the cold and give plenty of food and shelter for other area winter wildlife as well.

ROCK-CAP FERNS

The snow we get in December tends to last. Such snows, during these days of limited daylight shortly before the solstice, did not get appreciated by many northlanders. But others, not just those who enjoy snow sports, found them valuable.

December's snowpack forms a blanket of cover that serves as a protection to the subterranean world. Not only does this help the critters wintering here, but also helps our pipes. Some of us remember all too well, those winters with little snow when many well and septic pipes freeze. What gets less attention at such times is that lots of hibernation frogs and snakes die in the cold as well.

Snow alleviates those hazards and makes coping with the coming cold easier for small mammals like shrews and mice as they go under the snow. And now the ruffed grouse is be able to hide in the snowpack too.

Not only do many animals do better once we get a snow cover of several inches to a foot, so do plants. Looking out on the landscape now, we see mostly bare, drab branches. The only apparent greens are the conifers. Other green plants are here too, but most are buried. About a month ago, we saw the mosses and clubmosses that remained green on the forest floor while the rest of the community lost this color for the season. They will stay green for the whole winter, but need this blanket of snow to keep from being too exposed to the cold. A few evergreen flowering plants — wintergreen and hepatica — are under covers too. We'll see them again in spring.

Recently, while walking among the rocks and cliffs by the St. Louis River at Jay Cooke State Park, I saw another plant that still is green and, though exposed to the air, will stay that color for months. Here on the sides of the rocks, I saw green ferns. Because of where they grow, these small ferns, only four to six inches tall, are known as rock-cap ferns (Polypodium).

I have seen them growing thickly on many rocky sites, usually on the top or the edge. They normally do not get coated with snow and so need to deal with winter conditions differently. The cold does not appear to hurt these hardy feather-shaped leaves, but the arid air of this season is hard on them. To cope with this dryness and to keep from desiccation, these ferns will curl their leaves. Warmer temperatures and moisture will cause them to open again.

In the states south of us grows a fern that is green the whole winter. Because of this greening in the cold, it is called Christmas fern. The rock-cap fern is our only evergreen fern and will remain green through the whole holiday season, when we often search for some green in the landscape.

WINTERGREENS

DESPITE THE CONDITIONS, whether there is snow cover or not, each year we look for some green and red in December. Frequently, we associate such colors with the American holly. This plant of sharp, coated, green leaves and clumps of red berries does fit that pattern, but American holly does not grow here. It is native to the south. (We do have a native holly found in the regions' swamps, but it tends to drop both the leaves and berries by December.) The same is true with poinsettia flowers we see so often now. This plant with its green and red leaves is also from the south, though cousins also do live here.

Lots of green still persists in the woods of the northland, however, and anyone out for a walk on these cold December days is quick to see this color in the drab scene. Most obvious are evergreen trees that abound in the north country. Though they have much green, they lack any red.

But there is more in the woods. Many downed logs, bases of trees and rocks are covered with any of several species of mosses. These small plants stay green in winter are easy to see with a lack of snow cover, but usually they are buried for the whole cold season.

On rocky cliffs, the rock-cap fern provides a bit of green, as does its cousins, the princess pines or clubmosses of the forest floor. But these non-flowering plants are also non-berrying. No red. For a green plant with red berries, we need to look among the leaves on the ground below the trees. During northland winters, several small plants survive the cold by keeping their green leaves. Hidden under the leaf litter and often a thick snowpack, they frequently go undetected by us. Some are best known by their flowers of spring and summer: hepatica, pyrola, and twinflower.

And nearby is a leafy plant known as wintergreen. With leaves also used for tea and gum, it is sometimes called teaberry, gumplant, or snowberry. Not only are the leaves tasty, like gum, but so are their red berries as well. Plants growing clusters of these red berries make for quite a green-red sight on the winter forest floor.

Last summer, the low-growing plants produced one-fourth inch white bell-shaped flowers. Pollinated by local bees, they produced red berries that came to our attention at about the time the leaves dropped from the nearby trees.

With red berries and shiny green leaves, the small plants continued through autumn. Now, in late December, those berries that did not catch the eye of passing hungry wildlife are still here in the woods. For those of us who desire to see some green and red now, we can search for these small wintergreens. Not as large as the American holly or poinsettia (and maybe under several inches of snow), they still show the green-red colors of the season.

GREAT GRAY OWLS

A S THE DEPTH OF WINTER SETTLES IN, subzero temperatures along with frequent snow become the norm. Local wildlife deals with this chill in several ways. Raccoons and skunks sleep through the coldest days. Voles and mice live in a network of tunnels beneath the snow. And ruffed grouse fly into drifts to fend off the cold. But many others go out each day to find needed meals to ward off the season. Birds devour seeds and suet from feeders. These foods satisfy them, while their presence satisfies us on long winter days.

But there are other birds with a different life style out there too. Raptors like hawks and owls cope with the winter in ways different from the birds that frequent our feeders. A few red-tailed hawks and northern goshawks stay with us through the duration of chilly times. These short days are spent trying to grab any unsuspecting birds and small mammals. Owls, such as the great horned owl and barred owl live with us all year and hunt through these long nights. Snowy backgrounds make prey stand out. Each year, some other owls from the far north also arrive for the winter. These winter visitors are usually of four kinds: great gray owl, northern hawk owl, snowy owl, and boreal owl. During some years, a few may be quite common (such as the winter of 2004-2005), but most of the time, sightings of these owls is an unusual treat.

A few years ago, the northland was host to large numbers of each of these species of owls (snowy owls were not as abundant as the others). With the snow cover at that time, many struggled to survive the cold. I remember driving a nearby route where I saw thirty-two great gray owls in one drive (sixteen were within a single mile). The following winters gave us fewer of these northern owls, but it at least some come every year.

Apparently, food availability on their home lands varies. During some lean years, the population of small rodents and hares in the far north wanes. At this time, the owls come to our region for meals. Most noticeable of the winter guests are the huge great gray owls. Two feet long with a wingspan of five feet, great grays reign as North America's largest owls. The gray-brown body has a long tail, a rounded head with rings around the yellow eyes and a black chin.

Although most great gray owls reside in the forests and bogs of Canada, some do nest in northern Minnesota. We seldom see them except in winter when they come into the open country to hunt. During these invasion years, we see many more than in a usual winter. Typically, we notice them perched on trees, posts or utility poles as we drive by. Such an impressive bird demands our attention, and more that one motorist has stopped for a longer look. The birds will often tolerate the presence of humans, allowing for us to observe them from parked cars or even to approach them on foot. To us they may look like they are merely resting at these elevated sites, but most likely, they are hunting. These huge owls have incredible hearing. They are able to determine the location of a mouse in its burrow more than a foot beneath the snow surface. In a silent flight, they plunge into the snow for their prey. Masses of fluffy feathers help to cushion the impact. Large plunge holes tell tales of their hunts, even if we do not see the hunter.

A FLOCK OF BOHEMIAN
WAXWINGS

DECEMBER 21 MARKS THE WINTER SOLSTICE, the first day of the winter season. Besides the beginning of the cold season, this date is also the one with the shortest daylight of the whole year. Sunrise is at 7:51 A.M. and the sun sets at 4:23 P.M. From now until late next June, the diurnal light will continue to lengthen. But cold and snow will persist for months.

Almost as regular as this change in the season are the annual Christmas bird counts. Begun about 1900 as a way of checking the populations of birds in our country, they have spread throughout the continent, and now thousands take place each year. Counters note the species of birds seen and how many within a specific area. With the large number of people doing the count, we can get a good look at the birds that winter with us.

By counting birds at this time, we are noting only the non-migratory birds, those staying here all year or those that have migrated to this region from further north. For these hardy birds, our home is their southern flight, and they remain here only for winter. Usually, by late December, wintering birds are settled in to stay. We may view many at our feeders without even leaving the heat of our house or out favorite chair. Those birds that do not come to the feeders need a more active search to locate. Some remain far back in the woods, along roadsides and fields, and a few find a good site in still-open water.

A few days ago, I had a visit from a flock of birds that will not appear at a bird feeder, but still came to my yard, Bohemian waxwings. The day was chilly and cloudy, not much wind made for good listening conditions. As I entered the backyard, I heard them. Their high-pitched twittering came from the site of our crab apple trees. A quick search revealed many — I estimated fifty — gray-brown birds with crests on their heads. A closer look showed a yellow band on the tip of the tail and a black mask across the eyes. I needed to get near them to see the small red wing patches that gave this group of birds the "waxwing" name. Early naturalists thought that these bright feathers looked like drops of wax used to seal letters at that time.

Each year we host cedar waxwings, smaller and more colorful than these northern cousins, in the summer. They frequently nest here, and we get used to their high whistles. As the season advances, they seek berries for food and can regularly be seen among the elderberries and cherries. Now that the cedar waxwings have gone, the Bohemian waxwings (also called "greater waxwings") come south from the far northwest. Elderberries and cherries are gone, but other fruits and berries, such as mountain-ash, highbush cranberries, hawthorns, and crab apples, are still here. The hungry flocks find them.

Flocks of waxwings usually remain for the whole winter, but need to move within the region to find ample food supplies. The birds are very gregarious, and the groups enlarge through the cold season. The flock of fifty I saw, sighted for the Christmas bird count, may mix with others later and make for a gathering of hundreds as we approach the end of winter. But for now, I'm glad to share the crab apples with such a loud and interesting group of birds.

THE DARK WEEK

WITH ALL THE HOLIDAY ACTIVITIES for December, it is easy to overlook or forget the natural happenings of this month. Typically, December is one of our colder months with an average temperature of about fourteen degrees. This invariably includes temperatures below zero that balance the occasional day of nearly forty degrees.

Though not our snowiest month, we do regularly get snowfalls, with an average of about fifteen inches. Once again, extremes exist, and we've seen them in the northland during the last few years. Snowfalls have varied from hardly any to about fifty inches during some recent Decembers. Nearly every year, we enjoy the holidays against a white background.

The most consistent natural event is neither of these weather notes, but instead it is the darkness. Among other names for this month is the "dark month." Though it appears to be unlikely for this time of year, December is the month of least daylight. Sunrises are late while sunsets are early. During the first two-thirds of the month, the days shrink in their lighted portions as we head towards the winter solstice. Once this milestone is passed, the days slowly begin to lengthen. The winter solstice, also known as the first day of winter, varies its date a bit, but is usually on or about December 21, and is known as the shortest day of the year. Amid chilly temperatures, the sunlight will show for only about eight and one-half hours, leaving fifteen and one-half hours of darkness.

A strange phenomenon happens during the second week of December. At this time, we experience the earliest sunsets of the year. Daylight exits at about 4:20 P.M. on each of these days and though we are still not at the solstice, the sunsets begin to be later each day after this time. With sunrises that are later each day as well, the days don't get longer until after the winter solstice. Sunrises continue to get later until the end of the month. After reaching the latest time of about 7:55 A.M., they finally become earlier in the new year, and we see longer days.

With the earliest sunsets of the year, it is easy to see why or how this time of December can be known as the dark week. Less daylight and more darkness can make for great sky and star watching, though. Quite a show now awaits those willing to take a chilly celestial view. Venus and Mars both are regular sky sights and frequently Jupiter and Saturn as we look after sunset or before sunrise. And as an added attraction, the Geminid meteor show of mid December is worth a look as well, anywhere from the tenth to the fifteenth.

Days are short and cold, but we are treated to dazzling late sunrises and early sunsets. With these and other sky watching, December's darkness is an interesting and dynamic step into winter.

Mountain-Ash Berries

T HIS TIME OF MID DECEMBER, we pass through the time of earliest sunsets for the whole year. During this dark time, culminating with the winter solstice on or about December 21, we have little daylight.

This first day of winter has least amount of daylight for the whole year. With late sunrises and early sunsets, we often commute to work in the dark and return with the aid of headlights. During such dark days, we try to see more in the light hours. Those of us who maintain bird feeders at this time see the diurnal activities of the avian visitors.

Chickadees, nuthatches, woodpeckers, and finches feed during the bright times of the day and rest in the darkness. With chilly temperatures and so many dark hours, they need to spend most of the daylight feeding. We see them gather seeds of various types at the feeders, but we don't see their meals elsewhere. Woodpeckers go for grubs in trees, chickadees and nuthatches seek small insects behind bark, and the finches find many seeds in fields and woods. And there's more.

Some birds select berries, even though they are frozen. Usually berry feeders do not come to visit us for their meals. Berries still available at this time include rosehips, highbush cranberries, crab apples, and mountain-ash. By far the most common of these winter berries most years is the mountain-ash. Anyone driving around the region is sure to see an abundance of these orange-red clusters hanging from many trees.

Years vary, but conditions were right for a huge berry crop during this season. Some northlanders say that the more mountain-ash berries there are, the colder the winter. Instead of being a sign of the coming season, their abundance is a testimony of the proper conditions of the past seasons.

The northland is home to three species of mountain-ashes, all of which hold these clusters of berries now. Common in the yards and city parks is the European or tame variety. Scattered in the rocky and hilly woods, we can find two native species. None of these are large trees. The unfortunate name of mountain-ash is a misnomer. Though perhaps, they will grow in mountains, they do well elsewhere too.

Even though the leaves are compound pinnate like the ash, they are not at all related to true ashes. Instead they are members of the rose family. And like many other members of this family, they put forth large attractive flowers. These flowers opened in late May and their white blossoms made us take note of them. During summer, the pollinated flowers developed berries, and after the leaves dropped in October, they got our attention.

Now in winter, they get noticed by more than us. Birds like grosbeaks, waxwings, and starlings consume these colorful winter foods, even though the berries are frozen. It's a long cold season to come, but mountain-ash berries will help many birds get through.

DECEMBER
DAILY CLIMATE INFORMATION FOR DULUTH, MINNESOTA

Normal Records

DAY	AVERAGE HIGH	AVERAGE LOW	RECORD HIGH	RECORD LOW	SUNRISE	SUNSET
1	27	14	54/1962	-24/1919	7:33	4:23
2	27	13	54/1962	-23/1976	7:34	4:22
3	26	13	55/1962	-20/1985	7:35	4:22
4	26	12	54/1941	-16/1991	7:37	4:22
5	26	12	52/1913	-13/1964	7:38	4:21
6	25	11	56/1939	-20/1972	7:39	4:21
7	25	11	51/1939	-26/1976	7:40	4:20
8	24	10	45/1990	-23/1932*	7:41	4:20
9	24	10	54/1939	-30/1876	7:42	4:20
10	24	9	46/1896*	-25/1977	7:43	4:20
11	23	9	53/1913	-27/1977	7:44	4:20
12	23	8	54/1891	-23/1879	7:45	4:20
13	23	8	52/1913	-23/1903	7:45	4:20
14	22	8	52/1894	-26/1901	7:46	4:20
15	22	7	48/1877	-25/1926*	7:47	4:21
16	22	7	50/1913	-28/1876	7:48	4:21
17	22	7	44/1939*	-21/1983*	7:49	4:22
18	21	6	48/1931	-32/1884	7:49	4:22
19	21	6	51/1923	-30/1983*	7:50	4:22
20	21	6	43/1923*	-34/1983	7:50	4:23
21	21	5	47/1894	-28/1989	7:51	4:23
22	20	5	50/1890	-22/1989*	7:51	4:24
23	20	5	49/1888	-30/1884	7:52	4:24
24	20	4	47/1881	-24/1933*	7:52	4:25
25	20	4	44/1999*	-34/1879	7:53	4:25
26	20	4	42/1908*	-27/1934	7:53	4:26
27	20	4	40/2003	-28/1924*	7:53	4:27
28	20	3	42/1896	-35/1917	7:53	4:28
29	19	3	46/1999	-30/1917	7:54	4:28
30	19	3	43/1901	-26/1938	7:54	4:29
31	19	3	49/1904	-31/1946	7:54	4:30

*Denotes latest of multiple years
Average Temperature for December: 14.8 F
Average Precipitation for December: 1.21 inches
Average Snowfall for December: 17.7 inches